Wow! Smart Grammar 2

집필진: 김미희, E·NEXT 영어연구회

김미희, 민문선, 민아현, 신가윤, 정민경, 정미정, Christina KyungJin Ham

김미희 선생님은 이화여자대학교 영어교육과를 졸업하고 EBS English에서 방영하는 'Yo! Yo! Play Time'과 'EBS 방과후 영어'를 집필 및 검토하셨으며, 베스트셀러인 '10시간 영문법'과 '영어 글쓰기왕 비법 따라잡기' 등의 많은 영어교재를 집필하셨습니다. E·NEXT 영어연구회는 김미희 선생님을 중심으로, 세계 영어교육의 흐름에 발맞추어 효과적이고 바람직한 영어 교수·학습 방법을 연구하는 영어교육 전문가들의 모임입니다.

Smart Grammar ②

지은이 김미희
펴낸이 정규도
펴낸곳 다락원

초판 1쇄 발행 2011년 9월 30일
초판 5쇄 발행 2017년 12월 20일

편집장 최주연
책임편집 장경희, 오승현
영문교정 Michael A. Putlack

아트디렉터 정현석
디자인 김은미, 윤미주, 이승현

다락원 경기도 파주시 문발로 211
전화: (02)736-2031 내선 510
Fax: (02)732-2037
출판등록 제1-2936호

Copyright ©2011 김미희

값 12,000원

ISBN 978-89-277-4022-3
      978-89-277-4024-7(set)

http://www.darakwon.co.kr
다락원 홈페이지를 통해 본책과 워크북의 영문 해석 자료를 받아 보실 수 있습니다.

출간에 도움 주신 분들

배정연(키다리교육센터 메인 강사)
전남숙(수지 키즈컬리지 원장)
Leigh Stella Lage(성남외국어고등학교 원어민교사)
이명수(덕소 아이스펀지 잉글리쉬 원장)
이선옥(OK's Class 원장)
박혜정(잉글루 고창 어학원 원장)
신은숙(플러스 공부방 원장)

내지 일러스트 안효순 **표지 일러스트** 노유이

Wow! Smart Grammar

2

Smart Grammar를 추천합니다!

외국어를 배우면서 실력을 한 단계 더 올리기 위해서는 문법 공부가 반드시 필요합니다. 하지만 생소한 문법 용어와 설명 때문에 많은 학생들이 문법을 어려워하지요. **WOW! Smart Grammar** 시리즈는 기존의 문법 교재와는 달리, 초등학생의 발달 단계와 영어 학습 능력에 맞추어 구성하였으며 문장 속에서 문법을 배우는 것이 큰 특징입니다. 억지로 문법에 꿰어 맞춰진 것처럼 지루한 예문이 아니라, 재미있는 스토리가 있는 생동감 넘치는 문장을 통해 문법을 자연스럽고 즐겁게 터득할 수 있는 살아있는 영문법 교재입니다.

이상민 (경희대학교 영미어학부 교수, 초중등 영어교과서 저자, EBS 방과후 영어 총괄기획)

영문법을 풀어가는 방식이 참신하고 재미있군요. 그런데 재미있다고 해서 저학년 위주의 가벼운 내용만 들어 있는 것이 아니라, 초등 영문법의 핵심 내용을 토대로 보다 심화된 중학교 기본 과정까지 다루고 있다는 점을 높이 평가합니다. 내용 구성이나 문제 유형 등 여러 면에서 영어교육 전문가 선생님들이 오랜 시간 동안 현장에서 직접 적용해보고 지도해 본 실제 경험이 고스란히 녹아 들어가 있다는 느낌이 듭니다. 또한 구성도 알차고, 워크북과 단어장까지 들어 있어 요즘 같은 자기주도학습 시대에 딱 맞는 교재라고 생각합니다.

이재영 (안양관악초등학교 교장, 경기도초등영어교육연구회 회장, 한국초등영어교육학회 부회장)

건물을 건축할 때 기초공사가 가장 중요하듯 이 책은 학생들의 영어 실력 향상을 위해 꼭 필요한 내용들을 좋은 구성을 통해 보여줌으로써 학생들에게 영어 학습의 튼튼한 기초를 제공해주고 있습니다. 또한 각 Unit마다 Story Grammar를 통해 윙키의 이야기 속에 녹아있는 문법적인 요소를 자연스럽게 추출해볼 수 있도록 한 점은 흥미를 잃지 않고 통합적으로 문법을 공부하며 영어 실력을 향상시키는 데 효과 만점이라고 할 수 있습니다.

이미현 (수내초등학교 교사)

부담스럽지 않은 구성에다 연습문제가 풍부해서 참 좋네요. 단순히 연습문제의 개수만 많은 것이 아니라 쉬운 문제부터 어려운 문제까지 차근차근 단계적으로 풀어볼 수 있게끔 구성되었고, 만화 등 여러 가지 다양한 상황들이 들어간 문제 유형들로 이루어져 있어 실제 아이들의 생활에서 활용될 수 있는 문법학습에 매우 효과적입니다.

최호정 (Brown International School 국제학교 BIS 서초캠퍼스 원장)

문법을 쉽고 재미있게 설명하고 있어서 좋고, 단계별·수준별로 구성된 연습문제와 워크북의 문제 등 풍부한 문제를 제공하고 있으며, 잘 정리된 단어장까지 완벽하게 준비된 교재입니다. 학원 교재로서는 선생님들의 일을 줄여준 고마운 교재이며, 또한 자기주도학습을 하기에도 좋은 교재라고 생각됩니다.

제니퍼 김 (English Hunters 원장)

영어를 배우면서 영문법에 어려움을 많이 느끼는 학생들이 대부분인데, **WOW! Smart Grammar**는 문법의 개념을 쉽고 친근감 있게 생활 언어로 설명해 주어서 아이들이 영문법의 기본 구조를 흥미 진진하게 이해하고 받아들일 수 있게 해주는 좋은 문법 지침서입니다. 각 Unit의 끝에 나오는 문화 관련 페이지도 형식적인 내용이 아니고 정성 들여 꾸며져서 재미있고 유익합니다.

유병희 (동백 정철어학원 원장)

사실 영문법을 가르치다 보면 아이들이 문법 용어와 표현을 어려워하는데요, **WOW! Smart Grammar**에서는 그런 문제점을 해결해주네요. 품사의 뜻과 문장의 구조 등 문법을 재미있게 설명해 주어서 좀더 접근하기 쉽게 되어 있어요. 또한 이 책은 실생활에서 쓰는 문장들을 예문으로 사용했기 때문에 문법을 문제풀이를 위해서만 공부하는 것이 아니라 배운 표현을 실생활에도 적용할 수 있게 해주네요.

이우리 (리버스쿨 분당 초등 전담 강사)

WOW! Smart Grammar will help students gain the confidence to improve their English ability. The book consists of guidelines that cover grammar, practice exercises, and activities which correlate with the national English textbooks used in public schools.

Puthea Sam (성남송현초등학교 원어민 교사)

WOW! Smart Grammar is a new and exciting book for young English learners. It uses a lot of imaginative scenarios to help kids understand the lessons. The unique fiction included is fascinating to young minds and serves to help motivate children to study. There are also a lot of nonfiction sections that are equally as interesting. All the activities included are fun and relevant to the book's curriculum. This book makes learning English enjoyable and easy. I recommend this book for anyone looking for a creative way to improve a child's English grammar.

Daniel Brown (서강대학교 외국어 교육대학원 전임 강사)

이 책의 구성과 특징

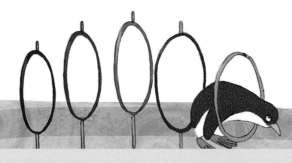

각 Unit별 주제에 맞는 실생활 속의 문장과 흥미로운 스토리로 문법을 익히고, 단계적으로 구성된 연습문제를 풀면서 실력을 다져 나갈 수 있도록 구성되어 있어요. 스토리는 연습문제에도 계속 연결되어 흐르기 때문에, 딱딱하고 지루한 문법을 공부하기 위해 문제를 푸는 것이 아니라 재미있는 스토리를 읽으면서 배운 문법 내용을 확인할 수 있어요. 초등 핵심 영문법뿐 아니라 중학 기초 영문법 내용도 미리 배울 수 있어요.

Unit별 핵심 정리
해당 Unit에서 학습할 중요 문법 내용이 무엇인지를 문장 속에서 풀어서 보여줍니다.

문법 설명
핵심 문법 내용을 이해하기 쉽게 풀어서 설명하고, 실생활에서 사용하는 다양한 문장을 통해 확인할 수 있도록 합니다.

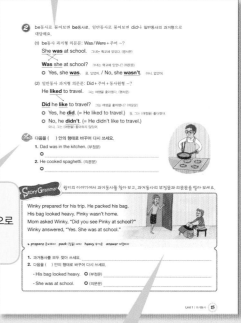

Check✔
앞에서 배운 핵심 문법 내용을 짧은 퀴즈 형식으로 간단하게 확인하고 넘어가는 코너로, 망각 곡선을 늦춰 기억력을 높여 줍니다.

Story Grammar
재미있고 흥미로운 스토리를 읽으면서 스토리 속에 녹아있는 문법 내용을 다지고 정리합니다.

기초 탄탄 Quiz Time
학습한 문법 내용을 점검하는 1단계 기초 문법 문제를 풀어봅니다. 앞 페이지에서 읽은 스토리는 이 코너의 문제들에서도 계속 이어집니다.

기본 튼튼 Quiz Time

한 단계 올라간 기본 문법 문제를 풀어봅니다.
이 코너에서도 스토리가 녹아 들어간 문제를 풀면서
배운 문법 내용을 확인합니다.

실력 쑥쑥 Quiz Time

기사, 만화, 일기 등 일상생활과 관련된 실용영어가
스토리 속에 녹아있는 심화된 문제를 풀면서
배운 문법을 최종 확인합니다.

Unit 꽉 잡기 Review Test

종합 문제를 풀면서 최종 점검 및 복습을 하는 코너입니다.
새롭게 바뀐 영어교과 교육과정의 개정 내용을 반영해서
장차 중학교의 중간·기말고사는 물론 각종 공인 영어 시험의
달라진 시험 유형에도 대비할 수 있도록 다양한 유형의
문제들로 구성하였습니다.

Super Duper Fun Time

해당 Unit과 관련된 영어권 문화 상식과 배경 지식을
즐겁게 습득할 수 있는 코너입니다.

별책부록: 워크북 & 단어장

핵심 문법 사항을 스스로 정리하고 다양한 연습문제를 풀어보면서
실력을 확실히 다질 수 있는 **워크북**과,
각 Unit에 나왔던 중요 단어와 문장을 한데 모아 다시 한 번 익힐 수
있는 깜찍한 사이즈의 **단어장**이 들어 있습니다.

| 1권 Unit 1~8 2개월 | + | 2권 Unit 1~8 2개월 | + | 3권 Unit 1~8 2개월 | = | 총 3권 6개월 |

WOW! Smart Grammar 시리즈는 전체 3권으로 구성되었으며,
각 권당 8개의 Unit으로 이루어져 있고, 한 Unit을 2차시에 걸쳐 수업할 수 있습니다.
WOW! Smart Grammar 1권부터 3권까지 일주일에 2번 수업할 경우 총 6개월 코스가 됩니다.

WOW! 아주 쉬운 문법 용어

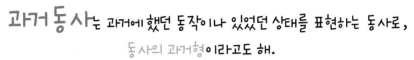

Hi! I'm Winky.

영문법은 어렵다고? 지금 고개 끄떡끄떡한 친구들은~

과거동사

과거동사는 과거에 했던 동작이나 있었던 상태를 표현하는 동사로,
동사의 과거형이라고도 해.
be동사를 비롯한 모든 동사는 다 과거형이 있어.
be동사의 과거형은 was나 were야.
일반동사 중에는 끝에 -ed 또는 -d만 붙이면
과거형 동사로 변신하는 것들이 있는데, 이런 경우를 규칙변화라고 하지.
하지만 아무 규칙 없이 불규칙적으로 변화하는 동사도 있어서,
슬프지만 이런 동사는 그냥 외울 수밖에 없어!

과거형 문장의 부정문은 어떻게 만들까?
be동사 과거형 문장의 부정문은 was나 were 뒤에 not을 붙이면 돼. 간단하지?!
그런데 일반동사 과거형 문장의 부정문을 만들려면 조동사 did가 필요해.
여기서 잠깐! 조동사란 '동사를 도와주는 보조 동사'야.
조동사 뒤에는 동사원형이 오지.
그럼 다시 일반동사 과거형 문장의 부정문으로 돌아와서,
조동사 do나 does의 과거형인 did 뒤에 not을 붙이고 동사원형을
쓰면 부정문이 완성돼.

과거형 문장의 의문문은
be동사나 조동사의 과거형을 주어 앞에 쓰고 문장 끝에
물음표를 붙여서 만들어. 의문문에 대한 대답은
be동사로 물어보면 be동사로, 일반동사로 물어보면
「did + 동사원형」이나 일반동사의 과거형으로 답하지.

과거동사 주어 ?

Go to ➜ Unit 1

일단 이걸 한번 읽어 봐!!

Hi! My name is Pinky.

현재진행형과 과거진행형

현재진행형은 '현재 ~하고 있다, ~하는 중이다'라는 뜻으로 지금 동작이 진행되고 있는 것을 의미해. 현재진행형 문장은 「be동사의 현재형(am, are, is) + 동사원형-ing」로 나타내면 돼. 여기서 잠깐! 동사원형에 -ing를 붙인 것을 현재분사라고 한다는 것도 기억해!

Go to Unit 2

과거진행형은 '(과거에) ~하고 있었다, ~하는 중이었다'라는 뜻으로 과거에 진행 중이던 것을 의미해. 「be동사의 과거형(was, were) + 동사원형-ing」로 쓰면 돼.

진행형 문장도 당연히 부정문이나 의문문으로 만들 수 있어. be동사의 과거형 뒤에 not을 붙이면 **진행형의 부정문**이고, be동사를 주어 앞으로 보내고 문장 끝에 물음표를 붙이면 **진행형의 의문문**이 되지.

형용사와 부사

명사나 대명사를 구체적으로 설명하거나 꾸며줄 때 필요한 것이 **형용사**야. an apple(사과 한 개)과 a delicious apple(맛있는 사과 한 개)을 보면 형용사 delicious의 역할을 알 수 있겠지?

부사는 동사, 형용사, 다른 부사, 문장 전체 등을 꾸며 줌으로써 어떤 동작이나 상황, 사건 등을 보다 구체적으로 나타내주는 말이야. He runs.(그가 뛴다.)보다는 He runs fast.(그가 빨리 뛴다.)라는 문장이 그가 '어떻게' 뛰는지 더 구체적으로 설명해 주지.

Go to Unit 3

비교급과 최상급

두 개 이상을 비교할 땐 비교급을 쓰는데, '내가 우리 셋 중에서 가장 잘생겼어.'처럼 세 개 이상의 사물이나 대상을 비교할 때는 뭘 쓸까? 바로 **최상급**을 쓰지.

두 개 이상의 사물이나 대상을 서로 비교할 때는 형용사나 부사의 모양을 바꿔서 나타낸다는 거 알아? 예를 들어, '내가 너보다 더 예뻐.'라고 할 때는 **비교급** 모양으로 써야 해. I'm prettier than you. 이렇게 말이지.

그러면 형용사나 부사가 비교급이나 최상급으로 변하기 전의 원래 형태는 뭐라고 부를까? 띵똥~! 맞았어, **원급**이라고 해.

Go to ▶ Unit 4

 ? ? 의문사

의문사는 사람이나 사물, 상황 등에 대해 물어볼 때 쓰는데, 의문대명사, 의문형용사, 의문부사 등이 있지. **의문대명사**는 문장에서 대명사 역할을 해. what(무엇), which(어느 것), who(누구, 누가), whose(누구의 것), whom(누구를) 같은 게 있어.

나... 좋아하는 사람 생겼어~ who?

의문형용사는 의문사가 명사를 수식하는 형용사 역할을 한다고 해서 붙여진 이름이야. What color do you like? (넌 무슨 색을 좋아하니?)의 What이 뒤의 명사 color를 수식하는 의문형용사야.

궁금한 게 있으면 의문사를 사용해서 물어봐~

의문부사는 시간, 장소, 방법, 이유 등을 물어볼 때 쓰는 의문사로 문장에서 부사 역할을 하지. when(언제), where(어디서), how(어떻게), why(왜) 같은 것들이 있어.

Go to ▶ Unit 5

비인칭주어 it과 There is/are ~

비인칭주어 it은 인칭주어가 아닌 it이라는 뜻이야.
주로 시간, 요일, 날짜, 날씨, 계절, 거리, 명암을 나타내지.
그럼, 인칭주어 it은 뭘까?? '그것'을 가리키는 3인칭 주어 it으로
'그것'이라고 해석하지.
하지만 비인칭주어 it은 특별히 해석을 하진 않아.

이상해...

'그것은' 다섯시야.

Dinky

Minky

There is ~나 There are ~ 구문은
'~이 있다'라고 할 때 쓰는 표현이야. There도 특별히
해석을 하진 않는다는 거 기억해! There is ~ 뒤에는 단수명사,
There are ~ 뒤에는 복수명사가 오지.

Go to Unit 6

전치사

시간, 장소, 위치, 방향, 수단, 방법 등을 나타내려면
전치사라는 게 필요해. 전치사는 보통 명사나 대명사 앞에 써.
이외에도 전치사는 be동사나 일반동사와 함께 묶여서
하나의 뜻을 나타내는 구를 만들기도 해.

Go to Unit 7

조동사 can과 will

앞에서 조동사가
먼저 잠깐 설명해 줬는데, 조동사가 뭐라고 했지?
동사를 도와주는 보조 동사라고 한 거 다들 잊지 않았지!
그럼 이 조동사 중에서 먼저 can과 will부터 알아보자.
can은 Yes, I can!(그래, 난 할 수 있어!)처럼
'가능'의 의미를 나타내고, will은 '미래'를 나타내.
참, 조동사는 문장에서 동사원형 앞에
위치한다는 것도 기억해 ~

내 앞으로 오렴.

can will
조동사 동사

Go to Unit 8

CONTENTS

과거동사

그럼, 일반동사의
과거형은 어떻게 만들어요?
과거형의 부정문과
의문문은요?

be동사의 과거형은
한 가지만 있는 게
아니란다.

☆ be동사의 과거형에는 was, were가 있어요.

☆ 일반동사의 과거형에는 규칙 변화를 하는 것과 불규칙 변화를 하는 것이 있어요.

Winky <u>was</u> on vacation. 윙키는 방학을 했다.
　　　　 is → was

He <u>went</u> on a trip to the USA. 그는 미국으로 여행을 갔다.
　　 go → went

☆ 과거형의 부정문과 의문문은 현재형의 부정문, 의문문과 같은 형태로 변해요.

Winky <u>was not</u> on vacation. 윙키는 방학을 하지 않았다.
　　과거동사의 부정문: 과거형 be동사＋not

<u>Did</u> he <u>go</u> on a trip to the USA? 그는 미국으로 여행을 갔니?
과거동사의 의문문: Did＋주어＋동사원형 ~?

be동사와 일반동사의 과거형

be동사의 과거형
am, is → was
are → were

1 과거동사는 '~이었다, ~했다'로 해석하며, 과거에 했던 동작이나 있었던 상태를 의미해요.

He is happy. 그는 행복하다. ○ He was happy. 그는 행복했다.
<u>현재형(~이다)</u>　　　　　　　　　　　　　<u>과거형(~이었다)</u>

2 일반동사에는 형태가 규칙적으로 변하여 과거형이 되는 동사와 불규칙적으로 변하여 과거형이 되는 동사가 있어요.

(1) 규칙 변화 동사 끝에 -ed 또는 -d를 붙여요.

I **work** hard. 나는 열심히 일한다. ○ I **worked** hard. 나는 열심히 일했다.
　　<u>현재형</u>　　　　　　　　　　　　　　　　<u>과거형</u>

동사	현재형	과거형	동사	현재형	과거형
대부분의 경우 동사 뒤에 -ed	work 일하다	work**ed** 일했다	「단모음+단자음」으로 끝나면 끝 자음을 한 번 더 쓰고 -ed	stop 멈추다	stop**ped** 멈췄다
e로 끝나는 동사는 뒤에 -d	like 좋아하다	like**d** 좋아했다	「자음+y」로 끝나면 y를 i로 바꾸고 -ed	cry 울다	cr**ied** 울었다

(2) 불규칙 변화 동사의 형태가 제각기 다르게 변해요.

He **comes** home. 그는 집에 온다. ○ He **came** home. 그는 집에 왔다.
　　<u>현재형</u>　　　　　　　　　　　　　　　<u>과거형</u>

현재형	과거형	현재형	과거형
go 가다 come 오다 do 하다 have 가지다	went 갔다 came 왔다 did 했다 had 가졌다	find 찾다 eat 먹다 leave 떠나다 fall 떨어지다	found 찾았다 ate 먹었다 left 떠났다 fell 떨어졌다

불규칙 변화 동사

현재형	과거형
make	made
sleep	slept
see	saw
write	wrote
get	got
take	took
wake	woke
meet	met
put	put
cut	cut
read	read
shake	shook

 과거동사에 동그라미 하고, 문장을 해석하세요.

He saw a map on the wall. ┈┈┈┈┈┈┈┈┈┈┈┈┈┈┈┈┈┈

be동사와 일반동사 과거형의 부정문과 의문문

주어에 따라 달라지는 be동사 과거형의 부정
· 주어 I, he, she, it: was not(= wasn't)
· 주어 we, you, they: were not (= weren't)

주어에 상관 없이 같은 일반동사 과거형의 부정
did not(= didn't) +동사원형

1 **(1)** be동사 과거형의 부정: was/were+not

She was home. 그녀는 집에 있었다. ○ She **wasn't** home. 그녀는 집에 없었다.
　　　　　　　　　　　　　　　　　　　　<u>was+not</u>

(2) 일반동사 과거형의 부정: 조동사 do/does의 과거형 did+not+동사원형

She went home. 그녀는 집에 갔다.

○ She **didn't go** home. 그녀는 집에 가지 않았다.
　　<u>didn't+동사원형</u>

be동사로 물어보면 **be**동사로, 일반동사로 물어보면 **did**나 일반동사의 과거형으로
대답해요.

(1) be동사 과거형 의문문: Was / Were + 주어 ~?

She **was** at school.　그녀는 학교에 있었다. (평서문)

Was she at school?　그녀는 학교에 있었니? (의문문)

○ Yes, she **was**.　응, 있었어. / No, she **wasn't**.　아니, 없었어.

(2) 일반동사 과거형 의문문: Did + 주어 + 동사원형 ~?

He **liked** to travel.　그는 여행을 좋아했다. (평서문)

Did he **like** to travel?　그는 여행을 좋아했니? (의문문)

○ Yes, he **did**. (= He liked to travel.)　응, 그는 (여행을) 좋아했어.

○ No, he **didn't**. (= He didn't like to travel.)
　아니, 그는 (여행을) 좋아하지 않았어.

 다음을 (　) 안의 형태로 바꾸어 다시 쓰세요.

1. Dad was in the kitchen. (부정문)

○ _____

2. He cooked spaghetti. (의문문)

○ _____

 윙키의 이야기에서 과거동사를 찾아 보고, 과거동사의 부정문과 의문문을 알아 보세요.

Winky prepared for his trip. He packed his bag.
His bag looked heavy. Pinky wasn't home.
Mom asked Winky, "Did you see Pinky at school?"
Winky answered, "Yes. She was at school."

❋ *prepare* 준비하다 *pack* (짐을) 싸다 *heavy* 무거운 *answer* 대답하다

1. 과거동사를 모두 찾아 쓰세요. _____

2. 다음을 (　) 안의 형태로 바꾸어 다시 쓰세요.

· His bag looked heavy.　○ (부정문) _____

· She was at school.　○ (의문문) _____

A 동사의 과거형을 쓰세요.

1. work ....
2. look ....
3. like ....
4. stop ....
5. cry ....
6. walk ....
7. study ....
8. answer ....
9. am ....
10. are ....
11. is ....
12. do ....
13. write ....
14. make ....
15. take ....
16. get ....

B ( ) 안의 동사를 과거형으로 바꾸어 빈칸에 쓰세요.

1. She .... to Central Park yesterday. (go)

2. It .... peaceful. (is)

3. They .... hungry. (are)

4. They .... lunch. (have)

5. The puppy .... hungry. (look)

6. They already .... lunch. (eat)

7. Dad .... some food with his magic. (cook)

부정문에 알맞은 말에 동그라미 하세요.

depressed 우울한
arrive 도착하다
nervous 긴장한

1. Winky (wasn't / weren't / didn't) in L.A.

2. They (wasn't / weren't / didn't) have much money.

3. They (wasn't / weren't / didn't) depressed.

4. Pinky (wasn't / weren't / didn't) get in the car.

5. She (wasn't / weren't / didn't) walk.

6. She (wasn't / weren't / didn't) tired.

7. Dad (wasn't / weren't / didn't) drive a car.

8. They (wasn't / weren't / didn't) arrive at a hotel.

9. They (wasn't / weren't / didn't) nervous.

 의문문에 알맞은 단어에 동그라미 하세요.

travel bag 여행 가방
pension
작은 호텔, 펜션

1. (Was / Were / Did) they in New York?

2. (Was / Were / Did) they happy?

3. (Was / Were / Did) he a student?

4. (Was / Were / Did) she go to school today?

5. (Was / Were / Did) they take an airplane?

6. (Was / Were / Did) there a travel bag?

7. (Was / Were / Did) they nervous?

8. (Was / Were / Did) they go to a hotel?

9. (Was / Were / Did) they arrive at a pension?

10. (Was / Were / Did) they rich?

Quiz Time
기본튼튼

 틀린 부분을 고쳐 올바른 과거형 문장으로 다시 쓰세요.

1. He were at Times Square yesterday.

   ➡ _____

2. He finded a fun place.

   ➡ _____

3. People was very busy.

   ➡ _____

4. They walkeed very fast.

   ➡ _____

5. He eated ice cream.

   ➡ _____

👀
Times Square
타임스 스퀘어 (뉴욕 시
의 중심부)
fun 재미있는; 재미

B 다음을 과거형 문장으로 바꾸어 다시 쓰세요.

1. She brushes her teeth.　➡ _____

2. I watch a movie.　➡ _____

3. I play baseball.　➡ _____

4. Steve meets his friends.　➡ _____

5. I cut the paper with scissors.　➡ _____

6. I read a book.　➡ _____

7. She is happy.　➡ _____

8. They go home.　➡ _____

👀
brush 닦다
teeth
tooth(치아)의 복수형
cut 자르다

C 다음을 부정문으로 바꿀 때 빈칸에 알맞은 말을 쓰세요.

1. They rode on an airplane again.

   ○ They _____ _____ on an airplane again.

rode
ride(타다)의 과거형

2. They talked to a girl.

   ○ They _____ _____ to a girl.

3. You moved from Korea.

   ○ You _____ _____ from Korea.

4. I was tired.

   ○ I _____ tired.

5. They arrived at the Grand Canyon.

   ○ They _____ _____ at the Grand Canyon.

D 다음을 의문문으로 바꾸어 다시 쓰세요.

1. He was thirsty.

   ○ _____

thirsty 목이 마른
experiment 실험
drinkable
마실 수 있는

2. The river was big and beautiful.

   ○ _____

3. Mom did an experiment.

   ○ _____

4. The water became drinkable.

   ○ _____

5. They were very happy.

   ○ _____

 A 윙키의 일기입니다. 밑줄 친 동사를 과거형으로 바꾸어 다시 쓰세요.

> leave 떠나다
> (과거형: left 떠났다)

Saturday, July 11   **Sunny**

I ¹⁾<u>wake</u> up at 8 o'clock.

I ²⁾<u>eat</u> breakfast very fast because I ³⁾<u>am</u> late.

My family ⁴⁾<u>leaves</u> our home at 8:30.

We ⁵⁾<u>go</u> from New York to L.A.

We ⁶⁾<u>are</u> very happy.

1. ➔ _____ 2. ➔ _____ 3. ➔ _____

4. ➔ _____ 5. ➔ _____ 6. ➔ _____

 B 그림을 보고, 보기에서 알맞은 것을 골라 과거형으로 바꿔 빈칸에 쓰세요.

> shake hands
> 악수하다

> make   live   dance   shake

1. The Indians _____ in a tent.

2. Winky _____ a fire.

3. Pinky _____ with Mom.

4. Dad and the leader _____ hands.

윙키의 하루 점검표입니다. 보기와 같이 질문에 답하세요.

exercise
운동; 운동하다
younger
(형제 중) 더 어린
sibling 형제 자매

☒ I did exercise in the morning.

○ I cleaned my room.

○ I didn't fight with my younger sibling.

☒ I washed my hands in the bathroom.

○ I wrote in my diary at night.

☒ I saved some money.

○ I had a wonderful day.

Did he do exercise in the morning?

○ No, he didn't do exercise in the morning.

1. Did he clean his room?

○ _____

2. Did he fight with his younger sibling?

○ _____

3. Did he wash his hands in the bathroom?

○ _____

4. Did he write in his diary at night?

○ _____

5. Did he save money?

○ _____

6. Did he have a wonderful day?

○ _____

Review Test
Unit 1 꽉 잡기

1. 다음 중 동사의 과거형이 <u>아닌</u> 것을 고르세요.

① was   ② did   ③ saw   ④ does

2. 다음 중 올바른 과거 문장을 고르세요.

① I am a student.
② I love my dogs.
③ I was happy yesterday.
④ I get up at seven o'clock.

3. 다음 우리말과 같은 뜻이 되도록 빈칸에 알맞은 단어를 쓰세요.

그녀는 음악을 들었어요.

○ She _____ to music.

4. 다음 중 과거 표현이 <u>틀린</u> 문장을 고르세요.

① I played basketball.
② I went to the gym.
③ He were late for school yesterday.
④ She watched a movie in the morning.

5. 다음 대화의 빈칸에 공통으로 알맞은 단어를 고르세요.

> A: I _____ my homework yesterday.
> B: You _____ a good job!

① do   ② did   ③ does   ④ are

6. 다음 중 빈칸에 알맞은 단어를 순서대로 바르게 짝지은 것을 고르세요.

> A: _____ he _____ home?
> B: Yes, he did.

① Do – go   ② Does – went   ③ Did – go   ④ Did – went

7. 다음 중 올바른 문장을 고르세요.

① We did not go there.   ② She did not has a doll.

③ He didn't does his best.   ④ You not did look beautiful.

8. 다음 중 A의 질문에 알맞은 대답을 고르세요.

> A: Was your mom home?
> B: _____

① Yes, she does.   ② No, she didn't.

③ Yes, she was.   ④ No, she weren't.

9. 다음을 과거 부정문으로 바르게 바꾼 것을 고르세요.

> The spaghetti looked very delicious.

① The spaghetti didn't look very delicious.

② The spaghetti looked not delicious.

③ The spaghetti not looked delicious.

④ The spaghetti didn't looked delicious.

10. 다음 중 <u>틀린</u> 문장을 고르세요.

① Did she go to the market?   ② I didn't watch TV.

③ Was you late for class?   ④ He didn't steal the bread.

유네스코 선정 세계문화유산

유네스코(UNESCO)에서는 1972년부터 보호할 가치가 큰 유적인 건축물, 장소 등을 '세계문화유산'으로 선정해서 관리하고 있어요. 미국의 세계문화유산을 몇 가지 구경해 볼까요?

그랜드 캐니언 국립공원 (Grand Canyon National Park, 1979)

지구에서 가장 큰 협곡으로 20억년 전에 생성되었대요.

You will be able to see the most powerful and inspiring landscape.

자유의 여신상 (The Statue of Liberty, 1984)

오른손에는 '세계를 비추는 자유의 빛'을 상징하는 횃불, 왼손에는 '1776년 7월 4일'이라는 날짜가 새겨진 독립선언서를 들고 있어요.

메사 베르데 (Mesa Verde, 1978)

콜로라도 주의 메사 평원지대에 있는 아나사지스 인디언족의 전통 주거지로, 8세기경부터 발전했어요.

Mesa Verde offers a spectacular look into the lives of the Indian.

*spectacular 장관을 이루는

현재진행형과 과거진행형

> 현재 진행 중인 일을
> 표현하듯 과거에 진행 중이었던
> 일도 표현할 수 있어!
> 어떻게 표현하는지
> 설명해 줄게.

> 에잉! 난 현재
> '놀고 있는' 중인데...

⚡ 현재진행형은 현재 진행 중인 일을 의미하며 「am / are / is +
동사원형-ing」로 표현해요.

Winky and Pinky are playing tennis now.
현재진행형(be동사의 현재형 + 동사원형-ing)

윙키와 핑키는 지금 테니스를 치는 중이다.

⚡ 과거진행형은 과거에 진행 중이었던 일을 의미하며 「was / were + 동사원형-ing」로
표현해요.

They were playing soccer. 그들은 축구를 하고 있었다.
과거진행형(be동사의 과거형 + 동사원형-ing)

현재진행형

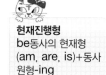

① 현재진행형은 현재 동작이 진행 중인 것을 의미하며 '~하고 있다, ~하는 중이다'로 해석해요.

Winky **is watching** TV.　윙키는 TV를 보고 있다.

② 현재진행형은 「be동사의 현재형(**am, are, is**)+동사원형-**ing**」로 나타내요. 동사원형에 **-ing**를 붙인 것을 현재분사라고 해요.

A baseball game **is playing** on TV.　TV에서는 야구 중계를 하고 있다.
　　　　　be동사의 현재형 + 동사원형-ing

● 현재분사 만드는 방법

동사	-ing 만드는 방법	예
대부분의 동사	동사 뒤에 -ing를 붙인다.	watch → watch**ing** study → study**ing**
e로 끝나는 동사	e를 빼고 -ing를 붙인다.	make → mak**ing** wave → wav**ing**
ie로 끝나는 동사	ie를 y로 바꾸고 -ing를 붙인다.	lie → l**ying** die → d**ying**
「단모음+단자음」으로 끝나는 동사	자음을 한 번 더 쓰고 -ing를 붙인다.	hit → hit**ting** run → run**ning**

③ 현재진행형의 부정문은 be동사 뒤에 **not**을 붙여서 만들어요.

Pinky **isn't**(= is not) **watching** TV.　핑키는 TV를 보고 있지 않다.
　　　be동사의 현재형 + not + 동사원형-ing

④ 현재진행형의 의문문은 주어 앞으로 be동사를 보내고 문장 끝에 물음표를 붙여요.

Are you **studying** English now?　너 지금 영어 공부하고 있니?
be동사의 현재형 + 주어 + 동사원형-ing ~?

Check 현재진행형에 동그라미 하고, 문장을 해석하세요.

1.  Are you studying now?　..

2. No. I am watching baseball.　..

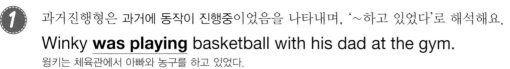 **과거진행형**

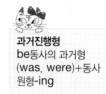
1 과거진행형은 과거에 동작이 진행중이었음을 나타내며, '~하고 있었다'로 해석해요.

Winky **was playing** basketball with his dad at the gym.

윙키는 체육관에서 아빠와 농구를 하고 있었다.

2 과거진행형은 「be동사의 과거형(was, were)+동사원형-ing」로 나타내요.

It <u>**was raining**</u> outside the window.   창 밖에는 비가 내리고 있었다.

　be동사의 과거형+동사원형-ing

3 과거진행형의 부정문은 be동사의 과거형 뒤에 **not**을 붙여요.

It <u>**was not snowing**</u> outside the window.   창 밖에는 눈이 오고 있지 않았다.

　be동사의 과거형+not+동사원형-ing

4 과거진행형의 의문문은 주어 앞으로 be동사의 과거형을 보내고 문장 끝에 물음표를 붙여요.

 <u>**Was**</u> it **raining** outside?   밖에 비가 내리고 있었니?

　be동사의 과거형+주어+동사원형-ing ~?

 Yes, it was raining.   네, 비가 내리고 있었어요.

Check 빈칸에 알맞은 be동사를 넣어 과거진행형 의문문을 만드세요.

1. .... you playing soccer?

2. .... he playing baseball?

 **Story Grammar**   동사의 현재진행형에 동그라미 하고, 밑줄 친 문장을 주어진 문장으로 바꿔 쓰세요.

Winky and his friend, Steve like baseball.

<u>They are playing baseball.</u>

Winky is throwing the ball.

Steve hits the ball and is running very fast.

* **throw** 던지다 **hit** 치다

1. 과거진행형 _____

2. 과거진행형의 의문문 _____

A 괄호 안의 동사를 현재진행형으로 바꾸어 빈칸에 쓰세요.

1. Winky _____ _____ a baseball game on TV. (watch)

2. A player _____ _____ at him. (look)

3. He _____ _____ Winky into the TV. (pull)

4. Winky _____ _____ in the baseball stadium. (stand)

5. The audience _____ _____ a big hand to him. (give)

6. He _____ _____ to them. (wave)

stadium 경기장
audience 관중
give a big hand 박수를 치다
wave (손을) 흔들다

B 현재진행형 부정문이 되도록 빈칸에 알맞은 단어를 쓰세요.

1. A batter _____ _____ hitting a ball.

2. A coach _____ _____ giving a signal to a player.

3. A pitcher _____ _____ throwing a ball.

4. A player _____ _____ running.

5. The audience _____ _____ sitting down.

6. A cheering squad _____ _____ dancing.

7. They _____ _____ starting the game.

batter 타자
coach 코치
give a signal 신호를 주다
pitcher 투수
throw a ball 공을 던지다
cheering squad 응원단

C 밑줄 친 부분을 과거진행형으로 바꿔 쓰세요.

1. Winky's family goes to the baseball stadium.

   ➲ _____

2. They are waiting in line to get tickets.

   ➲ _____

3. They are watching the baseball game from their seats.

   ➲ _____

4. The pitcher is throwing the ball.

   ➲ _____

5. The second baseman is running very fast.

   ➲ _____

6. The audience is screaming.

   ➲ _____

wait in line
줄을 서서 기다리다
scream
괴성(비명)을 지르다

D 과거진행형 의문문이 되도록 빈칸에 알맞은 be동사를 쓰세요.

1. _____ they watching the baseball game?

2. _____ they standing up?

3. _____ the pitcher throwing the ball?

4. _____ the batter holding a bat?

5. _____ a player sliding into the second base?

6. _____ a cheering squad clapping?

7. _____ the audience clapping?

hold a bat
방망이를 잡다
slide 슬라이딩하다
second base 2루
clap 박수 치다

A 괄호 안의 동사를 현재진행형 부정으로 바꾸어 빈칸에 쓰세요.

1. I ＿＿＿＿ ＿＿＿＿ ＿＿＿＿ basketball at the basketball stadium. (watch)

2. The players ＿＿＿＿ ＿＿＿＿ the national anthem. (sing)

3. Five players ＿＿＿＿ ＿＿＿＿ basketball. (play)

4. The other players ＿＿＿＿ ＿＿＿＿ on the bench. (sit)

5. A player ＿＿＿＿ ＿＿＿＿ a ball. (shoot)

> basketball stadium 농구경기장
> sing the national anthem 애국가를 부르다
> shoot a ball 공을 던지다

B 현재진행형 문장을 의문문으로 바꾸어 쓸 때 빈칸에 알맞은 말을 쓰세요.

1. One player is passing the ball.

   ➡ ＿＿＿＿ the ball?

2. The referee is blowing his whistle.

   ➡ ＿＿＿＿ his whistle?

3. The coach is shouting at the players.

   ➡ ＿＿＿＿ at the players?

4. The players are going to the bench.

   ➡ ＿＿＿＿ to the bench?

5. They are drinking water.

   ➡ ＿＿＿＿ water?

> pass the ball 공을 패스하다
> referee 심판
> blow a whistle 호루라기를 불다

보기에서 알맞은 동사 골라 과거진행형으로 바꾸어 문장을 완성하세요.

| hit | give | enter | watch | pass |

enter the field
경기장으로 들어오다
warning 경고

1. Winky's family _____ _____ the World Cup.

2. The soccer players _____ _____ the field.

3. One player _____ _____ the ball to another player.

4. The player _____ _____ the ball with his hand.

5. The referee _____ _____ the player a warning.

D 보기에서 알맞은 동사를 골라 과거진행형으로 바꾸어 문장을 완성하세요.

| do | sleep | rain | play |

1
_____ you _____ outside at two in the afternoon?

2
No. It _____ _____ at that time. So I couldn't play outside.

3
Then what _____ you _____?

4
I _____ _____ on the sofa.

Unit 2 | 현재진행형과 과거진행형   **31**

 다음을 현재진행형으로 바꾸어 문장을 다시 쓰세요.

1. Winky and Pinky play soccer with their family.

   ➡ ....

2. Winky runs toward the goal.

   ➡ ....

3. He kicks the ball.

   ➡ ....

4. Dad blocks the ball.

   ➡ ....

> kick the ball
> 공을 차다
> block the ball
> 공을 막다

 다음을 보기처럼 바꾸어 쓰세요.

> Steve is playing soccer.
>
> ➡ 부정문   Steve isn't playing soccer.
>
> ➡ 의문문   Is Steve playing soccer?
>
> ➡ 과거진행형   Steve was playing soccer.

1. Dinky is running toward Mom.

   ➡ 부정문 ....

   ➡ 의문문 ....

   ➡ 과거진행형 ....

2. Dinky is holding a ball in his mouth.

   ➡ 부정문 ....

   ➡ 의문문 ....

   ➡ 과거진행형 ....

윙키가 친구 Steve와 주고 받은 문자 메시지를 보고, 물음에 답하세요.

take a rest
휴식을 취하다
plan 계획을 세우다
hurt one's leg
다리를 다치다

Hi, Steve. What are you doing now?

Hi. I'm doing my homework.
How about you?

I'm taking a rest.
I'm planning to play tennis with my sister.
Can you join us for a game?

I was playing tennis with my dad at 8:00 A.M.
I hurt my leg.
So I can't join you.

Oh, I'm sorry to hear that.

1. What is Steve doing?

> ....

2. Is Winky doing his homework, too?

> ....

3. Was Steve playing tennis with Winky?

> ....

4. What is Winky planning to do?

> ....

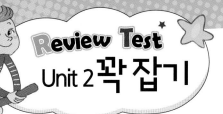

1. 다음 중 동사를 **-ing** 형태로 <u>잘못</u> 바꾼 것을 고르세요.

① make – making   ② come – coming

③ study – studing   ④ play – playing

2. 다음 중 빈칸에 알맞은 말을 고르세요.

> Winky _____ swimming in the pool.

① are   ② is   ③ does   ④ doesn't

3. 다음 빈칸에 공통으로 알맞은 말을 고르세요.

> · _____ you working right now?
>
> · _____ they cooking?

① Are   ② Is   ③ Do   ④ Don't

4. 다음 중 현재진행형 부정문을 바르게 나타낸 것을 고르세요.

① He wasn't lying on his bed.

② They weren't eating cookies.

③ I'm not going home yesterday.

④ You are not riding a bike.

5. 다음 의문문에 알맞은 답을 고르세요.

> Is she driving right now?

① Yes, he is.   ② Yes, she does.

③ No, she isn't.   ④ No, she doesn't.

6. 다음 중 밑줄 친 **be동사**가 <u>잘못된</u> 것을 고르세요.

① I <u>was</u> playing basketball with my friend.

② It <u>was</u> raining all of a sudden.

③ We <u>were</u> running toward the house.

④ We <u>was</u> waiting for the rain to stop.

7. 다음 중 빈칸에 알맞은 말을 순서대로 바르게 짝지은 것을 고르세요.

> A: _____ you playing tennis at 1:30?
>
> B: No, I _____ .

① Am – am not   ② Are – are not

③ Was – wasn't   ④ Were – wasn't

8. 다음 중 올바른 문장을 고르세요.

① They are working yesterday.

② They doesn't listening to music.

③ They weren't wearing their uniforms.

④ They is watching TV.

9. 다음을 현재진행형으로 바꿔 다시 쓰세요.

1) They jump. ➲ ....

2) She was watching them. ➲ ....

10. 다음을 부정문으로 바꿔 다시 쓰세요.

1) He is running very fast. ➲ ....

2) I was shaking hands with her. ➲ ....

모든 동사는 진행형이 가능하다?!

'나는 연필을 2개 가지고 있는 중이다.' 혹은 '나는 기분이 좋은 중이다.'라고 하면 어색하죠? 이처럼 '알다'와 관련된 동사(know, understand, imagine, believe, remember), '소유하다'와 관련된 동사(have, belong, need, cost), 감정과 감각을 나타내는 동사(like, love, want, feel, see, smell)는 진행형으로 쓰지 않아요.

단, have가 뒤에 오는 명사와 함께 행동을 나타낼 때는 진행형으로 쓸 수 있어요.

have가 '~을 가지다'라는 소유의 뜻일 때는 진행형을 못 쓰지만…

'시간을 보내다'라는 뜻일 때는 진행형으로 나타낼 수 있는 거지!

형용사와 부사

형용사와 부사는 문장의 내용을 더 풍요롭게 꾸며준대!

맞아! 그럼, 형용사와 부사에는 어떤 것이 있는지 볼까?

⭐ 형용사는 명사 또는 대명사를 꾸며주거나 설명해주는 역할을 해요.

Look at the big box. 큰 상자를 봐라. (명사 수식)
형용사 ──→ 명사

The box is big. 그 상자는 크다. (주어 설명)
명사 ◄─── 형용사

⭐ 부사는 동사, 형용사, 다른 부사, 문장 전체 등을 꾸며주는 역할을 해요.

Winky is very happy. 윙키는 매우 행복하다. (형용사 수식)
부사 ──→ 형용사

형용사의 종류와 용법

1 형용사는 사람이나 사물의 성질이나 상태를 나타내는 말로, 숫자, 날씨, 색깔, 맛 등이 이에 속해요. 형용사에는 kind, tall, special, happy, angry, one, two, first, second, windy, cold, sweet 등 여러 단어들이 있어요.

Today is sunny.　오늘은 날씨가 화창하다.

Winky eats the delicious cake.　윙키가 맛있는 케이크를 먹는다.

형용사의 용법
- 제한적 용법:
  형용사+명사,
  (-thing)명사+
  형용사
- 서술적 용법:
  be동사+형용사

-thing+형용사
something
beautiful (아름다운
어떤 것)
something cold
(차가운 어떤 것)

2 형용사는 문장 속에서 두 가지 용법으로 쓰여요.

(1) **제한적 용법** 형용사가 명사 앞이나 뒤에 와서 명사를 꾸며주는 역할을 해요. 주로 명사 앞에 와서 「형용사+명사」의 순서로 꾸며주지만, -thing으로 끝나는 명사는 뒤에서 꾸며줘요.

He buys beautiful flowers.　그는 아름다운 꽃을 산다.

　　　　형용사+명사 (형용사 beautiful이 뒤에 나오는 명사 수식)

※어떤 꽃인지 형용사 beautiful이 꾸며주고 있어요.

(2) **서술적 용법** 주로 be동사 뒤에 와서 주어의 상태를 설명해줘요. 이 경우에는 「be동사+형용사」의 순서로 쓰여요.

The party is fun.　그 파티는 재미있다.

　　　　be동사+형용사 (이다+재미있는 = 재미있다)

※주어인 '파티'가 어떠한지 형용사 fun이 설명해주고 있어요.

Check 형용사를 찾아 괄호 안에 쓰고, 그 용법을 빈칸에 쓰세요.

1. The book is interesting. (　　　　　　　)　.............................

2. The red flowers are beautiful. (　　　　　　)　.............................

부사의 종류와 위치

little은 형용사로
'작은'의 뜻으로 쓰이
기도 해요.
a little은 '약간'의
의미를 가져요.

1 부사는 어떤 일이 언제, 어디서, 어떻게, 얼마나 자주 일어나는지 등을 설명해줘요.

종류	부사
때	now 지금　yesterday 어제　today 오늘
장소	here 여기　there 거기　near 근처에　far 멀리
방법	fast 빠르게　slowly 천천히　quickly 빨리　well 잘　hard 열심히
정도	very 매우　much 많이　little 조금　too 너무

2 부사는 동사, 형용사, 다른 부사, 문장 전체 등을 꾸며주는 역할을 해요.

(1) 부사는 동사를 꾸며줘요.

He studies hard.   그는 열심히 공부한다.
동사 ┗━━━┛ 부사

(2) 부사는 형용사를 꾸며줘요.

His friends are very excited.   그의 친구들은 매우 신났다.
부사 ┗━━━┛ 형용사

(3) 부사는 다른 부사를 꾸며줘요.

I love my friends very much.   나는 나의 친구들을 매우 많이 사랑한다.
부사 ┗━━━┛ 부사

(4) 부사는 문장 전체를 꾸며줘요.

Luckily, his friends remember his birthday.
부사 ┗━━━━━━━━━━┛ 문장

운 좋게, 그의 친구들이 그의 생일을 기억하고 있다.

※ 대부분 「형용사+ly」는 부사가 돼요. 하지만 형용사와 부사 모양이 같은 경우도 있죠.

beautiful 아름다운 + **ly** ❍ **beautifully** 아름답게

fast 빠른 (형용사) / 빠르게 (부사)   **hard** 어려운 (형용사) / 열심히 (부사)

very와 much
둘 다 부사이고 very가 much를 꾸며줘요.

형용사가 「자음+y」로 끝나면 y를 i로 고치고 -ly를 붙여요.
happy
→ happi+ly
❍ happily 행복하게

③ 빈도부사란 얼마나 자주 일어나는지를 나타내는 부사를 말해요. 빈도부사는 일반동사 앞, 조동사 뒤 또는 be동사 뒤에 놓여요.

Winky always gets up at eight.   윙키는 항상 8시에 일어난다. (일반동사 앞)

It is sometimes rainy here.   여기는 때때로 비가 온다. (be동사 뒤)

주요 빈도부사
always 항상
usually 보통
often 종종
sometimes 때때로
never 전혀 ~ 아니다

 부사에 동그라미 하세요.

Pinky studies English very hard. She is often late for school.

 윙키의 이야기에서 형용사와 부사를 찾아 쓰세요.

It is Winky's birthday. Winky's friends throw a birthday party for him. He gets many presents, so he is very happy. He quickly opens a big green box. There is a long new magic wand in the box.

* **throw a birthday party** 생일파티를 열다   **magic wand** 마법 지팡이

1. 형용사 ....

2. 부사 ....

 A 형용사를 찾아 동그라미 하고, 뜻을 쓰세요.

1. It was a small room. ....

2. Winky was sleeping in his old bed. ....

3. His friends gave him ten presents. ....

4. He was around many presents. ....

5. But that was his sweet dream. ....

6. He is very excited about his birthday. ....

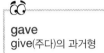

gave
give(주다)의 과거형

 B 밑줄 친 형용사의 용법을 쓰세요.

1. Today is <u>sunny</u>. ....

2. Pinky and her friends gather on the <u>big</u> playground.

   ....

3. They talk about his <u>exciting</u> birthday. ....

4. Let's throw a surprise party! It sounds <u>fun</u>. ....

5. Let's bake a <u>delicious</u> cake, too. ....

6. That's <u>great</u>. ....

7. Let's talk about some <u>special</u> presents for Winky.

   ....

형광펜 쫘~악

형용사와 함께 쓰이는 동사
아래 동사들의 바로 뒤에
형용사가 오면 어떤 뜻이
되는지 알아두세요.
look ~처럼 보이다
feel ~라고 느끼다
smell ~한 냄새가 나다
taste ~한 맛이 나다
sound ~처럼 들리다

부사를 찾아 동그라미 하고, 뜻을 쓰세요.

1. Let's go to the magic shop quickly. ....

2. They happily go to the magic shop together. ....

3. Does he like to read books much? ....

4. He sometimes reads books. ....

5. His magic wand is old now. ....

6. He wants a magic cape very much. ....

quickly 재빨리
together 함께

 밑줄 친 부사가 꾸며주는 곳을 찾아 보기와 같이 표시하세요.

> Let's wrap his presents now.

wrap 포장하다
ribbon 리본
quietly 조용히

1. Pinky makes a pretty ribbon <u>very</u> well.

2. Make the ribbon <u>quickly</u>, Pinky.

3. Wait! I'm making the ribbon <u>fast</u>.

4. Everyone, talk <u>quietly</u>, please.

5. Winky <u>usually</u> gets home early.

6. <u>Luckily</u>, he is cleaning the classroom at school.

 틀린 부분을 찾아 고쳐서 문장을 다시 쓰세요.

1. Pinky decorates her room with balloons twenty today.

   ➡ ....

   decorate 장식하다

2. They bake delicious something.

   ➡ ....

   형광펜 쫘~악

   -thing으로 끝나는 명사는
   형용사가 뒤에서 꾸며줘요.

3. She buys flowers beautiful.

   ➡ ....

4. She is very excited about his birthday party big.

   ➡ ....

5. They quickly wrap Winky's present with two ribbons red.

   ➡ ....

B 단어나 구를 바르게 배열하여 문장을 완성하세요.

1. my Pinky sister is kind

   ➡ ....

2. delicious This birthday cake is

   ➡ ....

3. bakes cookies She sweet

   ➡ ....

4. Fifteen beautiful are red and yellow flowers

   ➡ ....

5. something buys A friend special

   ➡ ....

C 괄호 안의 부사를 어순에 맞게 넣어 문장을 다시 쓰세요.

take an exam
시험을 치다
celebrate 축하하다

1. Everyone takes an English exam. (often)
   ➡ _____

2. They study English very hard. (always)
   ➡ _____

3. Winky is very excited to study English. (usually)
   ➡ _____

4. His friends celebrate his birthday. (never)
   ➡ _____

5. They talk each other in English. (sometimes)
   ➡ _____

D (   ) 안의 단어를 문장에 맞게 바꾸어 빈칸에 쓰세요.

hide and seek
숨바꼭질

1. Pinky said _____ , "Let's play hide and seek at my home!" (happy)

2. She talks to her friends _____ . (quiet)

3. Winky feels bad. They play _____ without him. (pleasant)

4. They _____ go home. (quick)

5. _____ , someone turns off the lights. (sudden)

6. Pinky _____ brings out Winky's birthday cake with candles on it. (slow)

 보기와 같이 두 문장을 한 문장으로 만드세요.

> Look at this candle! It's big. ◐ Look at this big candle!

1. Here is your birthday hat. It's blue.

   ◐ ....

2. They are balloons. There are twenty.

   ◐ ....

3. Here is your plate. It is round.

   ◐ ....

4. Winky eats cookies. They are delicious.

   ◐ ....

B 부사 much, well, perfectly, fast를 사용해 문장을 완성하세요.

perfectly 완벽하게
hide 숨기다

1. You sing the happy birthday song very _____.

2. This is for you. I ran very _____ to get that.

3. This is a magic cape! I can hide myself _____!

4. Thank you very _____.

C 틀린 부분을 찾아 바르게 고쳐 문장을 다시 쓰세요.

1. Let's play the piñata game quick.

   ➲ ....

2. It's Winky's turn. Winky careful covers his eyes.

   ➲ ....

3. He hits the piñata very hardly with a stick.

   ➲ ....

4. Sudden, the piñata breaks and they get some sweet candy.

   ➲ ....

piñata
피냐타 (미국 아이들이
파티 때 눈을 가리고 막대
기로 쳐서 터트리는, 장난
감과 사탕이 가득 든 통)

turn 순서

cover 가리다

D 윙키의 일기를 읽고, 물음에 답하세요.

Thursday, May 26   ☀ Sunny

Today was my birthday. My friends threw a surprise party.
Pinky slowly brought out my birthday cake.
They baked cookies, too. I ate five cookies!
I got a long new magic wand and a magic cape.
We played the piñata game. It was a perfect birthday.

brought
bring(가지고 오다)의
과거형

1. How was the weather?

   ➲ ....

2. How many cookies did Winky eat?

   ➲ ....

3. What presents did Winky get?

   ➲ ....

Review Test
Unit 3 꽉 잡기

1. 다음 설명 중 틀린 것을 고르세요.

① 형용사는 명사를 꾸며준다.
② 부사는 다른 부사를 꾸며줄 수 있다.
③ 빈도부사는 be동사 뒤에 놓인다.
④ something은 형용사가 앞에서 꾸민다.

2. 다음 중 형용사 용법이 다른 것을 고르세요.

① Your hat is great.
② The boy is very kind.
③ I eat a delicious cake.
④ That jacket is nice.

3. 다음 중 밑줄 친 부사의 성격이 다른 것을 고르세요.

① I quickly put on my clothes.
② She often goes to the library.
③ He usually reads a book.
④ I always wake up at 7 o'clock.

4. 다음 중 부사의 위치가 잘못된 것을 고르세요.

① Suddenly, she cries.
② They always open the window.
③ It sometimes is windy.
④ I never go back.

5. 다음 중 빈칸에 공통으로 알맞은 것을 고르세요.

· Run _____ ! You are late!
· You are a _____ runner.

① very   ② fast   ③ slowly   ④ wonderful

6. 다음 중 빈칸에 공통으로 알맞은 것을 고르세요.

> · Her sister is very _____ .
>
> · She speaks English a _____ .

① cute   ② little   ③ much   ④ lot of

7. 다음 중 밑줄 친 단어가 꾸며주는 것을 잘못 표시한 것을 고르세요.

① It is a nice day today.

② He has brown hair.

③ Bring the boxes carefully.

④ She can speak English very well.

8. 다음 중 틀린 문장을 고르세요.

① She plays soccer well.

② He works very hardly.

③ My friend loudly calls me.

④ She walks very quietly.

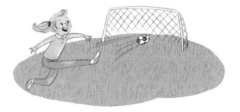

9. 그림을 보고, 빈칸에 들어갈 수 없는 것을 고르세요.

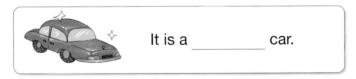

It is a _____ car.

① blue   ② new   ③ big   ④ quickly

10. 그림을 보고, 빈칸에 들어갈 수 없는 것을 고르세요.

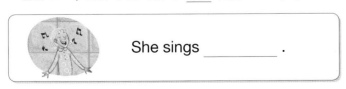

She sings _____ .

① well   ② careful   ③ very hard   ④ nicely

미국 친구들의 생일 파티

Let's play the piñata game!

piñata(피냐타)는 멕시코의 전통 민속놀이로 생일파티 때 많이 하는 게임인데, 우리나라의 '박 터뜨리기'와 비슷해요. 다양한 색깔의 종이로 만든 '박' 속에 사탕과 과자, 장난감 등을 넣어 두어요. 이것을 나뭇가지나 높은 곳에 매단 후에 눈을 가리고 막대기로 쳐서 터뜨리는 거예요.

Pack your bags for a birthday pajama party.

미국에서는 생일 주인공이 친구들을 집으로 초대해서 밤늦게까지 함께 놀아요. 친구들과 음식을 해 먹고 같이 게임도 하면서 한 방에서 같이 잠을 자요. 때로는 방에 텐트를 치고 자기도 해요. 재미있겠죠?

비교급과 최상급

어때, 내 키가 더 크지?
이렇게 비교하는 표현에는
비교급과 최상급이 있어.

그럼 어떻게
표현하는지 한번 볼까?

우힛!

⭐ 형용사와 부사의 모양을 바꿔서 비교급과 최상급을 만들 수 있어요.

stronger 더 힘센   **strongest** 가장 힘센
　　비교급　　　　　　　　　　최상급

more expensive 더 비싼   **most expensive** 가장 비싼
　　비교급　　　　　　　　　　　　최상급

⭐ 비교급은 둘을 비교할 때 쓰이며, 최상급은 셋 이상에서 가장 뛰어난 것을 말할 때 쓰여요.

Winky is taller than her.   윙키는 그녀보다 키가 크다.
　　　　비교급을 활용한 문장

Winky is the tallest.   윙키가 가장 키가 크다.
　　　　최상급을 활용한 문장

형용사와 부사의 비교급과 최상급

1 형용사와 부사의 비교급은 '…보다 더 ~한'의 의미로 둘 사이를 비교할 때 쓰여요. 비교급과 최상급을 만드는 방법은 형용사와 부사의 길이(음절 수)나 형태에 따라 달라져요.

비교급(더 ~한)			예
규칙 변화	1음절 단어	형용사/부사+er	tall → tall**er**　high → high**er** old → old**er**　hard → hard**er**
		자음+y → y를 i로 바꾸고 -er	heavy → heav**ier**　easy → eas**ier** pretty → prett**ier**　hungry → hungr**ier**
		단모음+단자음 → 자음 한 번 더 쓰고 -er	fat → fat**ter**　big → big**ger** hot → hot**ter**
	2음절 이상 단어	more+형용사/부사	careful → **more** careful beautiful → **more** beautiful quickly → **more** quickly
불규칙 변화		good/well → **better**　bad/badly → **worse** many/much → **more**　little → **less**	

2 형용사와 부사의 최상급은 '가장 ~한'의 의미로 셋 이상에서 최상인 것을 의미할 때 쓰여요.

최상급(가장 ~한)			예
규칙 변화	1음절 단어	형용사/부사+est	tall → tall**est**　high → high**est** old → old**est**　hard → hard**est**
		자음+y → y를 i로 바꾸고 -est	heavy → heav**iest**　easy → eas**iest** pretty → prett**iest** hungry → hungr**iest**
		단모음+단자음 → 자음 한 번 더 쓰고 -est	fat → fat**test**　big → big**gest** hot → hot**test**
	2음절 이상 단어	most+형용사/부사	careful → **most** careful beautiful → **most** beautiful quickly → **most** quickly
불규칙 변화		good/well → **best**　bad/badly → **worst** many/much → **most**　little → **least**	

 비교급은 동그라미, 최상급은 별표하고 그 뜻을 쓰세요.

1. old / older / oldest ....

2. smaller / smallest / small ....

비교급과 최상급의 활용

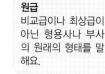

비교급 and 비교급
더욱 더 ~, 갈수록 점점 더 ~
Winky is gaining more and more weight. (윙키는 점점 더 살이 찌고 있다.)

원급
비교급이나 최상급이 아닌 형용사나 부사의 원래의 형태를 말해요.

1 비교급(둘 중 하나가 '…보다 더 ~한')은 둘 사이를 비교할 때 쓰이며, 뒤에 **than**이 와요.

주어＋동사＋비교급＋than＋명사／대명사: (둘 중에서) …보다 더 ~한

Winky is **heavier than** Pinky. 윙키는 핑키보다 더 무겁다.

2 원급을 활용한 비교는 동등한 사람이나 사물을 비교할 때 써요.

주어＋동사＋**as**＋원급＋**as**: …만큼 ~한

Dinky weighs **as much as** Minky. 딩키는 밍키만큼 무게가 나간다.

3 최상급('가장 ~한')은 셋 이상에서 최상인 것을 의미할 때 쓰이며, 최상급 앞에는 **the**를 붙여요.

주어＋동사＋**the**＋최상급(＋명사): 가장 ~한

Winky's dad is **the heaviest** in his family.
윙키 아빠는 가족 중에서 가장 체중이 무겁다.

 비교급이 쓰인 문장에는 '비', 최상급이 쓰인 문장에는 '최'라고 쓰세요.

1. Dinky drinks more milk than Minky. ....

2. Dinky's glass is the biggest. ....

 비교급을 찾아 동그라미 하고, 밑줄 친 문장을 최상급으로 바꿔 쓰세요.

Winky is taller than Pinky. So ¹⁾Winky has a longer jump rope.
Winky's cap is expensive, but ²⁾Pinky's cap is more expensive.
Mom's training pants are shorter than Dad's training pants.
The whole family exercises together.

＊*jump rope* 줄넘기; 줄넘기 하다

1. ◯ ....

2. ◯ ....

Quiz Time 기초탄탄

 A 그림을 보고, 알맞은 비교급에 동그라미 하세요.

1.

more expensive / cheaper

2.

longer / shorter

3.

smaller / bigger

4.

more / less

5.

cleaner / dirtier

6.

thinner / thicker

7.

heavier / lighter

8.

lower / higher

형광펜 쫘~악

비교급을 만드는 규칙
• 1음절인 형용사나 부사 뒤에는 -er을 붙인다.
• y로 끝나는 형용사나 부사는 y를 i로 바꾸고 -er을 붙인다.
• 「단모음+단자음」으로 끝나는 형용사나 부사는 끝자음을 하나 더 붙인 뒤 -er을 붙인다.
• 2음절 이상인 형용사나 부사는 그 앞에 more를 붙인다.

cheap (값이) 싼
– cheaper 더 싼
thin 가는, 마른
– thinner 더 가는, 더 마른

B 최상급의 형태가 맞으면 동그라미, 틀리면 ×표 하세요.

1.

the tallest ....

2.

the fastest ....

3.

the most furthest ....

4.

the most flexible ....

5.

the fattest ....

6.

the strongest ....

형광펜 쫘~악

최상급을 만드는 규칙
• 1음절인 형용사나 부사 뒤에는 -est를 붙인다.
• y로 끝나는 형용사나 부사는 y를 i로 바꾸고 -est를 붙인다.
• 「단모음+단자음」으로 끝나는 형용사나 부사는 끝자음을 하나 더 붙인 뒤 -est를 붙인다.
• 2음절 이상인 형용사나 부사는 그 앞에 most를 붙인다.

further (거리가) 먼
flexible 유연한

C 비교급 표현이 알맞은 것에 동그라미 하세요.

1. She is (fatter / fater) than her mom.

2. Her mom is (more beautiful / beautifuler) than her.

3. He sweats (most / more) than her.

4. Pinky walks (as faster as / as fast as) Winky.

5. Badminton is (easier / more easy) than tennis.

6. Jump rope is (as hard as / harder) running.

7. Dinky is (happyer / happier) than Minky.

8. His dad is not (as old as / as older as) his grandfather.

D 최상급 표현이 알맞은 것에 동그라미 하세요.

1. She is the (youngest / younger) in her family.

light 가벼운
popular 인기 있는
among ~ 중에서

2. He is the (most light / lightest) among his friends.

3. His dad is the (strongest / stronggest) in his family.

4. Mom is the (talest / tallest) in her family.

5. He is the (most / more) handsome in his class.

6. Dad is the (fatest / fattest) in his family.

7. She is the (most popular / popularest) in her class.

8. Pinky's hair is the (shortest / most short) among her friends.

 보기에서 알맞은 단어를 골라 빈칸에 알맞게 바꿔 쓰세요.

> slow   long   fast

1

I am _____ than you.

Am I _____ than you? No way!

2 Right. You are _____ than me. Catch up with me!

3 Hehehe~~. I am _____ than you.

4 No. I win. You are _____ than me.

I win.

FINISH

 밑줄 친 부분을 바르게 고쳐 빈칸에 쓰세요.

1. This gym is <u>the largeest</u> one in our neighborhood.

   ○ This gym is _____ one in our neighborhood.

2. Fitness is <u>the most cheap</u> exercise.

   ○ Fitness is _____ exercise.

3. Yoga is <u>the more interestingest</u> exercise.

   ○ Yoga is _____ exercise.

4. The yoga trainer is <u>the thinest</u> person in the gym.

   ○ The yoga trainer is _____ person in the gym.

gym 체육관
neighborhood
이웃, 농네
fitness 운동, 헬스
yoga 요가

C 단어나 구를 바르게 배열하여 완전한 문장을 만드세요.

treadmill 러닝머신
sportswear 운동복
Pilates 필라테스

1. than Pinky at the gym Winky arrives earlier

   ❍ _____ .

2. more A treadmill is expensive a bike than

   ❍ _____ .

3. Pinky's sportswear is Winky's than newer

   ❍ _____ .

4. fun Yoga is as Pilates as

   ❍ _____ .

D 보기에서 알맞은 단어를 골라 빈칸에 비교급 또는 최상급 형태로 바꾸어 쓰세요.

> happy   popular   good   much   warm

Tomas: Today is _____ than yesterday.

Winky: I like this weather. I am _____ than yesterday.

Tomas: Good. I'm also happy.

Winky: Did you watch the soccer game on TV yesterday?

Tomas: Yes, I did. I like Park Jisung.

He is the _____ player on the Korean team.

Winky: I know. But I like Ahn Junghwan _____ than him. I think he is the _____ _____ player in Korea.

 A 보기와 같이 두 문장을 합쳐서 한 문장으로 만드세요.

> A dumbbell is heavy. A barbell is heavier.
>
> ○ A barbell is heavier than a dumbbell.

dumbbell 아령
barbell 역기
ocean 바다, 대양
vaulting pole
장대높이뛰기 봉

1. A volleyball is big. A basketball is bigger.

○ ....

2. Baseball is popular. Soccer is more popular.

○ ....

3. The swimming pool is cold. The ocean is colder.

○ ....

4. A stick is long. A vaulting pole is longer.

○ ....

B 보기의 단어를 알맞게 바꿔 넣어 반대되는 문장을 쓰세요.

> hot   young   short   boring

boring 지루한

1. Today is the coldest day of the year.

○ ....

2. He is the tallest boy in his class.

○ ....

3. P.E. is the most fun class today.

○ ....

4. She is the oldest teacher at my school.

○ ....

이야기를 읽고, <u>틀린</u> 부분을 모두 찾아 바르게 고쳐 쓰세요.

Winky's family is watching a home shopping advertisement. A man on a treadmill runs more fast than a woman on a different treadmill.

The treadmill is the expensivest health machine. They say if we buy a treadmill, they will give us a bike.

The bike is more smaller than the treadmill. The woman show host is very thin.

Dad's tea is hoter than Mom's coffee. So Dad drinks slowest than Mom.

1. _____ ➡ _____

2. _____ ➡ _____

3. _____ ➡ _____

4. _____ ➡ _____

5. _____ ➡ _____

1. 다음 중 원급과 비교급이 바르게 연결된 것을 고르세요.

① fast – more fast   ② hot – hoter

③ happy – happier   ④ popular – more popularer

2. 다음 중 원급과 최상급이 바르게 연결되지 <u>않은</u> 것을 고르세요.

① fat – fattest   ② young – youngest

③ exciting – most exciting   ④ heavy – heavyest

3. 다음 중 빈칸에 알맞은 비교급의 형태를 고르세요.

> Winter is _____ fall.

① colder   ② more cold than

③ colder than   ④ much cold than

4. 다음 중 빈칸에 알맞은 최상급의 형태를 고르세요.

> Which mountain is the _____ in the world?

① highhest   ② highest

③ most high   ④ much more highest

5. 다음 중 올바른 문장을 고르세요.

① The bird is as bigger as the fly.

② The bird is more big than the fly.

③ The bird is bigger than the fly.

④ The bird is big than the fly.

6. 다음 중 올바른 문장을 고르세요.

① This red sports car is most expensive car in our country.

② This red sports car is the most expensive car in our country.

③ This red sports car is the expensivest car in our country.

④ This red sports car is the most expensivest car in our country.

7. 다음 중 표에 대한 설명으로 올바른 것을 고르세요.

	나이	몸무게	키	시력(좌 / 우)
Mike	10	35	138	(1.5 / 1.5)
Robin	13	47	156	(0.9 / 0.7)
Lucy	12	42	144	(2.0 / 1.5)
Katie	11	33	135	(0.1 / 0.1)

① Lucy is younger than Mike.

② Robin is the shortest of the four.

③ Katie's eyesight is better than Lucy's.

④ Robin is the heaviest of the four.

8. 완전한 문장이 되도록 바르게 연결하세요.

1) America is further away　·　　　　　·　than meat.

2) Vegetables are healthier　·　　　　　·　than Japan.

9. 세 학생들의 성적표를 보고, (　　) 안의 단어를 활용해서 빈칸을 완성하세요.

	Sujin	Sam	Sue
Math	85	92	93
English	88	92	98

1) Sam is ＿＿＿＿＿ at math ＿＿＿＿＿ Sujin. (good)

2) Sue is the ＿＿＿＿＿ student of the three. (smart)

10. 단어를 바르게 배열하여 완전한 문장을 만드세요.

1) higher Baekdu Mountain than is Halla Mountain

➡ ＿＿＿＿＿＿＿＿＿＿＿＿＿＿＿＿＿＿＿＿＿ .

2) class Tom handsome is his the most in

➡ ＿＿＿＿＿＿＿＿＿＿＿＿＿＿＿＿＿＿＿＿＿ .

The Keys to Having a Healthy Body

건강한 몸을 만들기 위해 할 수 있는 운동에는 어떤 것들이 있으며
그것의 영어 이름은 무엇일까요? 여러분에게 맞는 운동을 찾아서 오늘부터 당장 시작해봐요.

Swimming vs Jogging

Jumping rope vs Using a hula hoop

Swimming burns more calories than jogging.

Jumping rope helps us lose more weight than using a hula hoop.

Yoga vs Pilates

Basketball vs Baseball

Yoga helps us become more flexible than Pilates.

Basketball helps us become taller than baseball.

의문사

영어로 질문할 때
쓰는 말이 있다며?

맞아. 의문사를 쓰지!
그럼, 어떤 의문사들이
있는지 한번 볼까?

★ 의문대명사는 사람이나 사물 등을 물어보는 의문사이고,
의문형용사는 의문사가 명사를 수식하는 역할을 해요.

Who is he? 그 남자는 누구죠?
의문대명사

Which room is he going to stay in? 그는 어느 방에서 지낼 거죠?
의문형용사 └──▲ (명사수식)

★ 의문부사는 시간이나 장소, 방법, 이유 등을 물어볼 때 쓰는 의문사로, when(언제),
where(어디서), how(어떻게), why(왜) 등이 있어요.

How long does it take from here to the airport?
의문부사

여기서 공항까지 얼마나 걸리나요?

의문대명사와 의문형용사

1 의문대명사는 사람이나 사물 등을 물어볼 때 쓰는 의문사로, 문장에서 대명사 역할을 하기 때문에 의문대명사라고 불러요. 의문사로 물어 볼 때는 yes나 no로 대답하지 않아요.

Who is he? 그는 누구인가요?

○ He's your cousin Willy. He's coming to our house.
  네 사촌 윌리란다. 그가 우리 집에 올 것이다.

2 의문대명사에는 **what**(무엇), **which**(어느 것), **who**(누구, 누가), **whose**(누구의 것), **whom**(누구를)이 있고, 「의문대명사+동사+주어 ~?」의 순서로 쓰여요.

What is this? 이것은 무엇이에요?

○ It's for Willy. 그것은 윌리에게 줄 것이다.

3 의문형용사는 의문사가 명사를 수식하는 형용사 역할을 해서 의문형용사라고 불러요.

Which room is Willy going to stay in? 어느 방에서 윌리가 지낼 거예요?
└─────→ 명사

○ He's going to stay in the room on the second floor.
  그는 2층 방에서 지낼 것이다.

4 의문형용사에는 「**what**(무슨 ~, 몇 ~)+명사」, 「**which**(어느 ~)+명사」, 「**whose**(누구의 ~)+명사」가 있고, 「의문형용사+명사+동사+주어 ~?」의 순서로 써요.

Whose pajamas are those? 저것은 누구의 잠옷인가요?

○ They're Willy's. 윌리 것이다.

● 의문대명사와 의문형용사 비교

의문사	의문대명사	의문형용사
what	**What** is this? 이것은 무엇입니까?	**What** kind of house do you live in? 당신은 어떤 종류의 집에서 삽니까?
which	**Which** is your car? 어느 것이 당신 차입니까?	**Which** color do you like, red or yellow? 어느 색을 좋아합니까, 빨간색 아니면 노란색?
who	**Who** is that man? 저 남자는 누구입니까? **Whose** is this? 이것은 누구의 것입니까? **Whom** do you like? 당신은 누구를 좋아합니까?	**Whose** bag is this? 이것은 누구의 가방입니까?

 의문대명사는 동그라미, 의문형용사는 세모표 하세요.

1. What time is Willy coming?

2. Whose is this bag?

 **의문부사**

1 의문부사는 시간이나 장소, 방법, 이유 등을 물어볼 때 쓰는 의문사로, 문장에서 부사 역할을 하기 때문에 의문부사라고 불러요.

When are you leaving? 당신은 언제 떠날겁니까?

◐ We are leaving in the afternoon. 우리는 오후에 떠날겁니다.

2 의문부사에는 **when**(언제), **where**(어디서), **how**(어떻게), **why**(왜)가 있고 「의문부사+동사+주어 ~?」의 순서로 써요. **how**는 형용사를 붙여 쓸 수도 있어요.

How long does it take to go to the airport? 공항까지 얼마나 걸립니까?

◐ It takes about one hour. 약 1시간 정도 걸립니다.

● **how와 형용사가 함께 쓰인 표현들**

How long does it take by airplane? (시간) 비행기로 얼마나 걸립니까?

How far is it from here to the airport? (거리) 여기서 공항까지는 얼마나 멉니까?

How old is he? (나이) 그는 몇 살입니까?

How many cookies are there in the box? (수) 그 상자 안에는 쿠키가 몇 개 있습니까?

How much is it? (양, 정도, 가치) 그것은 얼마입니까?

 의문부사에 동그라미 하세요.

1. Where is Willy?

2. How old is his dad?

 밑줄 친 문장이 대답이 되도록 빈칸에 의문사를 넣어서 의문문을 완성해 보세요.

Winky's cousin is coming today.
¹⁾He lives in New Zealand. He is coming by plane.
He is arriving at 6 o'clock. ²⁾Winky's family is going
to the airport to pick him up at 4:30.
Winky's dad is driving the car to the airport.

✽ *arrive* 도착하다 *pick up* (차를) 태우러 가다, 마중나가다

1. _____ does he live?

2. What _____ does Winky's family go to the airport to pick him up?

알맞은 의문대명사에 동그라미 하세요.

(Who / What / Which) is calling Winky's dad?

   ◐ Willy is calling him.

(Who / What / Which) wants to visit Winky's house?

   ◐ Winky's cousin wants to visit his house.

(Who / What / Which) does he hang up?

   ◐ He hangs up the phone.

(Whom / What / Which) did Winky's dad tell his family?

   ◐ Winky's dad told the good news to his family.

보기에서 알맞은 단어를 골라 의문형용사 뒤에 넣어 문장을 완성하세요.

time	room	book	kind	food

What _____ does Willy arrive?

   ◐ He arrives at 6 o'clock in the evening.

What _____ of book is that?

   ◐ It's a travel book.

Whose _____ is this?

   ◐ That's Willy's book.

Whose _____ is he going to stay?

   ◐ He's going to stay in Winky's room.

Which _____ does he like, Korean or Western food?

   ◐ He likes both.

- who는 사람, 신분, 관계를 물을 때 사용해요.
- what은 사물을 묻거나 직업을 물을 때 사용해요.
- whom은 목적격 의문사예요. 하지만 실제 말할 때는 whom 대신 who를 많이 써요. **who(m)** do you like? (너는 누구를 좋아하니?)

hang up 전화를 끊다

stay 머무르다

4

C 단어나 구를 바르게 배열하여 완전한 문장을 만드세요.

magic marble
마법 구슬
look at ~을 보다
rub 문지르다
cast a spell
주문을 외우다

1. Why take out did Winky a magic marble?

윙키는 왜 마법 구슬을 꺼냈나요?

○ Because he was trying to look at Willy.

2. did Winky do What with the magic marble?

윙키는 마법 구슬로 무엇을 했나요?

○ He rubbed the marble while casting a spell.

3. in the marble? Where was Willy

구슬 안에서 윌리는 어디에 있었나요?

○ He was in the airplane.

D 밑줄 친 부분이 올바른 문장은 동그라미, 틀린 문장은 ×표 하세요.

1. How long did they wait for Willy? ....

○ They waited for Willy for 10 minutes.

wait 기다리다

형광펜 쫘~악

How often은 「의문부사
＋부사」의 형태로 '얼마나
자주'라는 뜻으로 쓰여요.

2. How far is he? ....

○ He is 19 years old.

3. How tall is he? ....

○ He's 185 cm tall.

4. How much bags does he bring? ....

○ He brings three bags.

5. How often does he visit Winky's house? ....

○ He visits Winky's house every two years.

 밑줄 친 부분에 관해 묻는 의문문을 만들 때 빈칸에 알맞은 의문사를 쓰세요.

next to ~ 옆에

1. <u>Willy</u> gets on the airplane.

   ◎ _____ gets on the airplane?

2. He puts his green bag <u>in the cabinet</u>.

   ◎ _____ does he put his green bag?

3. He talks to <u>a girl</u> sitting next to him on the airplane.

   ◎ _____ does he talk to?

4. He drinks <u>juice</u>.

   ◎ _____ does he drink?

 보기에서 알맞은 말을 골라 빈칸에 넣어 이야기를 완성하세요.

What time   Whose   Which

1. _____ does the airplane arrive?
   It arrives at 5:50.

2. _____ games do you like, board games or online games?
   Um, I...

3. Excuse me. _____ would you like to eat, chicken or fish?
   I would like chicken.

4. _____ video game is that?
   Oh, it's mine. I like that game.

C 다음을 보기처럼 의문문으로 바꾼 후에 의문부사를 사용해서 다시 쓰세요.

> Winky's family goes out to pick him up at 4:30.
>
> ○ Does Winky's family go out to pick him up at 4:30?
>
> ○ When does Winky's family go out to pick him up?

1. They are taking the car to the airport.

   ○ _____ they taking the car to the airport?

   ○ _____ _____ they taking to the airport?

2. They are waiting for Willy at the arrival hall.

   ○ _____ they waiting for Willy at the arrival hall?

   ○ _____ _____ they waiting for Willy?

3. Dad waves to Willy.

   ○ _____ Dad wave to Willy?

   ○ _____ _____ Dad wave to?

D 틀린 부분을 찾아 고쳐 문장을 다시 쓰세요.

1. What big is the bag?

   ○ _____

2. How much clothes does he have?

   ○ _____

3. How far does he stay at Winky's house?

   ○ _____

4. How many money does he exchange?

   ○ _____

 핑키의 일기를 보고 대답을 알 수 있는 의문문에는 동그라미, 알 수 <u>없는</u> 의문문에는 ×표 하세요.

> Willy came to my house today.
>
> We went to the airport by car at 4 o'clock.
>
> We waited for Willy at the arrival hall.
>
> Dad waved to Willy. I'm happy because Willy came.

1. Who came to Pinky's house? ....

2. How did Pinky's family go to the airport? ....

3. Where is Willy from? ....

4. How long was Willy on the airplane? ....

 윌리가 입국 심사를 받고 있습니다. 빈칸에 알맞은 의문사를 넣어 완성하세요.

occupation 직업
purpose 목적
visit 방문; 방문하다
plan 계획하다
relative 친척

1 _____ are you from?

I'm from New Zealand.

2 _____ is your occupation?

I'm a student.

3 _____ is the purpose of your visit?

I'm visiting my relatives.

4 _____ are you planning to stay?

I'm planning to stay at my relatives' house.

윌리가 작성한 입국 신고서와 세관 신고서에 코코아가 쏟아져 글씨가 보이지 않는 곳이 생겼습니다. 안 보이는 곳에 있던 질문을 완성해 다시 쓰세요.

Arrival Form   Name: Willy Watson

1. ⬛⬛⬛ you live?

I live in New Zealand.

2. ⬛⬛ your occupation?

I'm a student.

3. ⬛⬛ you staying in Korea?

I'm staying in Korea for 15 days.

Did you visit any other countries before arriving in Korea?   I visited Japan.

4. ⬛⬛ do you come to Korea?

Once every 2 years.

5. Why ⬛⬛ come to Korea?

I'm here to visit my relatives.

1. _____

2. _____

3. _____

4. _____

5. _____

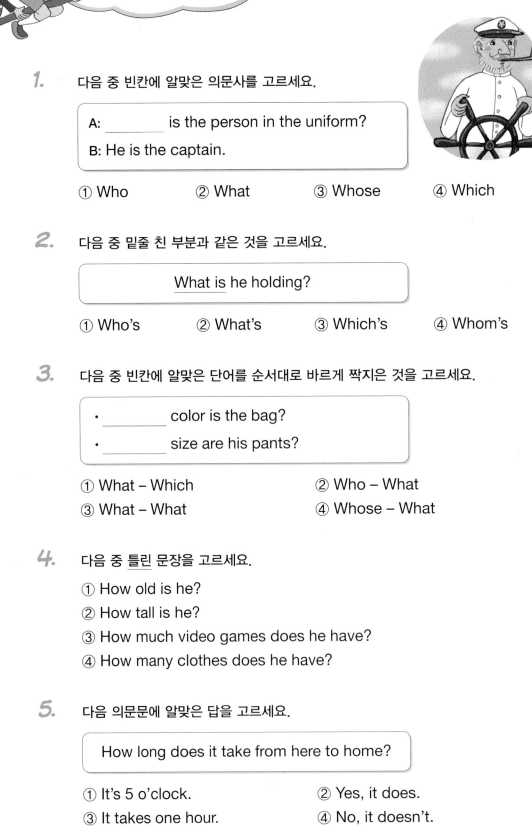

1. 다음 중 빈칸에 알맞은 의문사를 고르세요.

> A: _____ is the person in the uniform?
> B: He is the captain.

① Who   ② What   ③ Whose   ④ Which

2. 다음 중 밑줄 친 부분과 같은 것을 고르세요.

> <u>What is</u> he holding?

① Who's   ② What's   ③ Which's   ④ Whom's

3. 다음 중 빈칸에 알맞은 단어를 순서대로 바르게 짝지은 것을 고르세요.

> • _____ color is the bag?
> • _____ size are his pants?

① What – Which   ② Who – What
③ What – What   ④ Whose – What

4. 다음 중 틀린 문장을 고르세요.

① How old is he?
② How tall is he?
③ How much video games does he have?
④ How many clothes does he have?

5. 다음 의문문에 알맞은 답을 고르세요.

> How long does it take from here to home?

① It's 5 o'clock.   ② Yes, it does.
③ It takes one hour.   ④ No, it doesn't.

6. 다음 중 빈칸에 알맞은 단어를 고르세요.

> How _____ is the hospital from here?

① much   ② far   ③ many   ④ often

7. 다음 중 빈칸에 공통으로 알맞은 것을 고르세요.

> · _____ often do you come here?
> · _____ many souvenirs are they buying?

① What   ② How   ③ Which   ④ Whose

8. 다음 중 올바른 문장을 고르세요.

① What are we meeting time?
② Which are gate you waiting?
③ Do how you go there?
④ How long does it take?

9. 그림을 보고, 빈 말풍선에 알맞은 질문을쓰세요.

10. 다음 우리말을 영어로 쓰세요.

1) 너의 생일은 언제니? ◐ ....

2) 그것은 얼마입니까? ◐ ....

공항에서 많이 쓰이는 영어표현은?

1 **Where is the check-in counter?** (탑승 수속장이 어디 있나요?)

요즘에는 안내 모니터를 통해서도 탑승 수속장을 확인할 수 있어요.

2 **Can I have your passport and ticket?** (여권과 항공권 주시겠어요?)

입국이나 출국할 때 가장 많이 듣는 표현이에요.

3 **Do you have any baggage to check?** (부칠 짐이 있나요?)

기내에 가지고 들어가지 못하는 짐이 있을 때는 "Yes, I have a bag."이라고 말하면 돼요.

4 **What's your final destination?** (최종 목적지는 어디인가요?)

입국 심사할 때 심사원이 물어보는 질문이에요.

비인칭주어 it과
There is / are ~

> 비인칭주어 it을 말하는구나! 시간, 요일, 날씨 등을 표현할 때 쓰는 '형식상의 주어'라는 거야.

> 날씨를 표현할 때 쓰는 주어가 따로 있다며?

⭐ 형식적으로 주어의 자리에 위치하는 비인칭주어 it은 우리말로 해석하지 않아요.

It's Sunday. 일요일이다.
요일을 나타내는 비인칭주어 it

⭐ '~이 있다'라는 뜻의 There is / are ~는 동사의 형태에 따라 뒤에 단수 또는 복수명사가 와요.

There is a tree. 나무가 있다.　**There are trees.** 나무들이 있다.
There is + 단수명사　　　　　　　　　　　There are + 복수명사

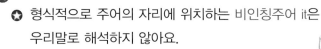

비인칭주어 it

비인칭주어 it
시간, 요일, 날짜, 날씨, 계절, 거리, 명암 등을 나타내요.

① 비인칭주어 it은 사람이나 사물을 가리키지 않으며, '그것'으로 해석하지 않아요.

(1) 인칭주어 it(그것) **It's a tree.**   그것은 나무이다.

(2) 비인칭주어 it   **It's fine today.**   오늘은 화창하다.

② 시간, 요일, 날짜, 날씨, 계절, 거리, 명암 등을 나타낼 때 쓰여요.

(1) 시간 **What time is it?** 몇 시입니까? ➡ **It's seven o'clock.** 7시 정각이다.

(2) 요일 **What day is it today?** ➡ **It's Sunday.**
오늘은 무슨 요일입니까?   일요일이다.

(3) 날짜 **What's the date today?** ➡ **It's April 22.**
오늘은 며칠입니까?   4월 22일이다.

(4) 날씨 **How's the weather today?** 오늘 날씨가 어떻습니까? ➡ **It's fine.** 맑다.

(5) 계절 **What season is it?** 무슨 계절입니까? ➡ **It's spring.** 봄이다.

(6) 거리 **How far is it?** 얼마나 멉니까? ➡ **It's about 2 miles.** 약 2마일이다.

(7) 명암 **Is it bright outside?** ➡ **It's bright outside.**
밖이 환합니까?   밖이 환하다.

 문장 속의 It이 비인칭주어로 쓰인 문장에는 동그라미, 그렇지 <u>않은</u> 문장에는 ×표 하세요.

1. It's warm outside. ....
2. It's fine today. ....
3. It's his hat. ....
4. It's very useful. ....

There is ~와 There are ~

① There is ~, There are ~ 구문은 '~이 있다'로 해석해요. 여기서 there는 따로 해석하지 않아요.

There is a can.   캔이 있다.
There is + 단수명사

※ 지시대명사 there(거기에): He's going **there**.   그는 거기에 간다.
거기에(지시대명사)

② There is ~ 뒤에는 단수명사, There are ~ 뒤에는 복수명사가 와요. 셀 수 없는 명사는 단수동사인 is 뒤에 오므로 양에 상관없이 「There is + 셀 수 없는 명사」로 써요.

There is + 단수명사
There are + 복수명사

구문 형태	예
There is+단수명사 (~이 있다)	**There is** a plate. 그릇이 있다. **There is** a cup. 컵이 있다. **There is** a lot of dust. 먼지가 많이 있다. (셀 수 없는 명사 dust)
There are+복수명사 (~들이 있다)	**There are** plates. 그릇들이 있다. **There are** cups. 컵들이 있다.

③ There is ~, There are ~ 구문의 부정문은 be동사 뒤에 부정의 **not**을 붙여요.

There isn't a broomstick. 빗자루가 없다.
= is not

There aren't any broomsticks. 빗자루들이 없다.
= are not

④ There is ~, There are ~ 구문의 의문문은 be동사와 there의 위치를 바꾸면 돼요.

Is there a mop? 대걸레가 있습니까?

Are there mops? 대걸레 여러 개가 있습니까?

 빈칸에 알맞은 단어를 쓰세요.

1. There _____ a trashcan. 쓰레기통이 있다.
2. There _____ a vacuum cleaner. 진공 청소기가 없다.
3. _____ _____ soap? 비누가 있나요?
4. _____ _____ many trashcans? 쓰레기통이 많이 있나요?

 윙키의 이야기에서 비인칭 주어와 There is/are ~ 구문을 찾아 보세요.

What's that sound? There is a washing machine
over there. Wow! It's very noisy. What day is it today?
It's Sunday. How's the weather? It's very sunny today.

* *sound* 소리 *washing machine* 세탁기 *noisy* 소란스러운

1. 밑줄 친 문장의 뜻을 쓰세요.

_____

2. 비인칭주어 it과 인칭주어 it을 모두 찾아 보세요.

• 비인칭주어 it이 쓰인 문장 _____

• 인칭주어 it이 쓰인 문장 _____

Quiz Time 기초탄탄

A 비인칭주어 it의 용법을 보기에서 골라 쓰세요.

| 시간 | 날씨 | 요일 | 날짜 | 거리 | 명암 | 계절 |

1. It's 8 o'clock. ....

2. It's spring. ....

3. It's April 22. ....

4. It is not far from here. ....

5. It's not raining now. ....

6. It was Saturday yesterday. ....

7. It's not dark here. ....

8. It's bright. ....

B it〔It〕이 비인칭주어이면 '비', 인칭주어이면 '인'이라고 쓰세요.

1. What time is it? ....

2. It's my trash. ....

3. Pick it up. ....

4. What day is it today? ....

5. It's Sunday. ....

6. It was a holiday yesterday. ....

7. It's not cold outside. ....

8. Can you push it? ....

C 알맞은 동사에 동그라미 하세요.

1. There (is / are) clothes in the box.

2. There (is / are) a can.

3. There (is / are) boxes on the side.

4. (Is / Are) there a glass in the box?

5. There (isn't / aren't) any plastic bottles.

6. There (isn't / aren't) any place to throw this away.

7. How many plastic bottles (is / are) there?

8. There (is / are) 5 plastic bottles.

9. There (is / are) a plastic box.

plastic 플라스틱

 D 알맞은 동사에 동그라미 하세요.

1. There (is / are) some water in the bottle.

2. (Is / Are) there a lot of dust on the desk?

3. There (is / are) 5 pieces of paper in the trashcan.

4. (Is / Are) there a basket?

5. There (is / are) some magical power.

6. There (is / are) paper in the basket now.

7. There (isn't / aren't) any paper in the trashcan.

dust 먼지
trashcan 쓰레기통
basket 바구니

 빈칸에 알맞은 말을 쓰세요.

1. When is the big cleanup?

   ➲ _____ on April 22.

2. What day is April 22?

   ➲ _____ Earth Day.

3. What day is it today?

   ➲ _____ Sunday.

4. What time is it?

   ➲ _____ 9 o'clock.

5. How's the weather?

   ➲ _____ not raining.

4.22 Earth Day

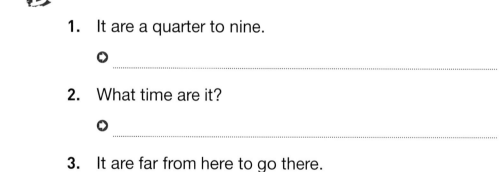 틀린 부분을 바르게 고쳐 문장을 다시 쓰세요.

1. It are a quarter to nine.

   ➲ _____

2. What time are it?

   ➲ _____

3. It are far from here to go there.

   ➲ _____

4. It are 1 mile from the event hall.

   ➲ _____

5. Are it windy?

   ➲ _____

형광펜 쫘~악

시간을 나타내는 방법
- ···분+to+~시:
  ~시 ···분 전
- ···분+before+~시:
  ~시 ···분전
- ···분+past+~시:
  ~시 ···분
- ···분+after+~시:
  ~시 ···분

C 빈칸에 알맞은 be동사를 쓰세요.

sign 표지판
restroom 화장실

1. There _____ not a lot of trees.

2. How many trees _____ there?

3. There _____ not even ten trees.

4. _____ there an event for Earth Day today?

5. Yes. There _____ a sign.

6. How many people _____ there?

7. There _____ more than 100 people.

8. _____ there a restroom close to here?

9. There _____ a restroom 500 meters from here.

 다음을 _____ 안의 문장으로 고쳐 다시 쓰세요.

cloud 구름
donate 기부하다

1. There isn't water in the event hall.

   ◯ 긍정문 _____

2. There is a cloud.

   ◯ 의문문 _____

3. There is a lot of water now.

   ◯ 의문문 _____

4. There are trees on the road.

   ◯ 부정문 _____

5. There is money to donate for Earth.

   ◯ 의문문 _____

A 윙키의 그림 일기를 보고, 빈칸에 알맞은 말을 쓰세요.

degree (온도 단위) 도
so far 아직까지는

1. .... raining now.

2. .... 26 degrees.

3. .... bright so far.

4. .... Thursday, July 7.

B 그림을 보고, 물음에 답하세요.

1. What season is it? ➡ ....

2. Is the weather nice? ➡ ....

3. What time is it? ➡ ....

4. Is it dark? ➡ ....

그림을 비교하며 뜻이 반대되는 문장을 완성하세요.

1. There _____ books   There aren't any _____
on the desk.   on the desk.

2. There _____ dust on   There isn't any _____
the computer.   on the computer.

3. There _____ any   There are two _____ .
chairs.

4. There _____ clothes   There aren't any _____
on the floor.   on the floor.

 보기처럼 빈칸을 채워 문장을 완성하세요.

Is there much water in Africa?

○ No, <u>there</u> <u>isn't</u> much water in Africa.

1. How many sick children are there in Africa?

○ _____ _____ many sick children in Africa.

2. Is there enough water in Africa?

○ No, _____ _____ enough water in Africa.

3. Is there a lot of food in Africa?

○ No, _____ _____ a lot of food in Africa.

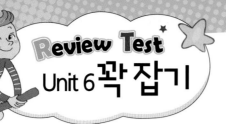

1. 다음 중 비인칭주어 it이 나타낼 수 <u>없는</u> 것을 고르세요.

① 시간   ② 날씨   ③ 거리   ④ 인칭

2. 다음 중 it의 쓰임이 <u>다른</u> 것을 고르세요.

① It is a book.   ② It is Sunday.

③ It is summer.   ④ What time is it now?

3. 다음 중 빈칸에 공통으로 알맞은 것을 고르세요.

- _____ is Sunday.
- _____ is 5 o'clock.

① That   ② She   ③ It   ④ They

4. 다음 중 뜻이 <u>다른</u> 것을 고르세요.

① It's one twenty-five.

② It's fifteen minutes before two.

③ It's a quarter before two.

④ It's one forty-five.

5. 다음 중 대화의 빈칸에 알맞은 것을 고르세요.

A: What's the _____ today?

B: It's April 5.

① date   ② day   ③ far   ④ time

6. 다음 중 빈칸에 알맞은 말을 순서대로 바르게 짝지은 것을 고르세요.

> A: How many books _____ there in the library?
>
> B: _____ are about 1,000 books.

① are – There ② be – That ③ is – There ④ does – There

7. 다음 중 올바른 문장을 고르세요.

① There is a egg.
② There is an cushion on the chair.
③ There are cars in the parking lot.
④ There are 28 desk.

8. 다음 중 빈칸에 알맞은 것을 고르세요.

> There are many _____.

① pens ② papers ③ sugars ④ a lot of water

9. 다음 중 밑줄 친 **There**(**there**)의 뜻이 <u>다른</u> 것을 고르세요.

① <u>There</u> are many books.
② The bathroom is over <u>there</u>.
③ <u>There</u> is a pencil case on the desk.
④ <u>There</u> is a bathroom next to the classroom.

10. 다음 중 올바른 문장을 고르세요.

① There are much cookies.
② There are waters in the glass.
③ There is full of dusts on the television.
④ There is a stationery store next to the market.

하나뿐인 지구를 지키자!

지구의 날 (Earth Day)

1970년 4월 22일 미국에서 많은 시민들이 모여 최초의 대규모 자연보호 캠페인을 벌인 날을 기념해서 제정되었어요. 해마다 이 날이 되면 전세계적으로 다양한 환경보호 행사가 열리지요. 미국 초등학교에서도 플라스틱 병으로 꽃병 만들기 등 재미있는 활동을 하며 환경에 대해 생각해 본답니다.

> It's Earth Day.
> Let's clean up the river.

> OK. Save our Earth. Loving Earth is loving yourself.

지구의 시간 (Earth Hour)

2007년 호주 시드니의 가정과 기업들이 한 시간 동안 전등을 끄면서 시작된 환경 희망 운동이에요. 1년에 하루, 딱 한 시간 동안만이라도 조명을 다 꺼서 에너지도 절약하고, 전기의 소중함도 다시 한번 깨달아 보자는 의미가 담겨 있지요. 우리나라에서도 매년 3월 26일 오후 8시 반부터 한 시간 동안 빌딩의 전등 불 끄기 운동을 하고 있어요.

> We have an event called Earth Hour. It's at 8:30 in the evening.

> Turn off the lights. Bow Wow!

전치사

전치사는 시간이나 위치, 방향 등도 나타낸대. 하나씩 살펴 보자.

위치를 표현할 때는 전치사라는 걸 쓰는 거지? 그런데 전치사는 위치만을 표현할까?

☆ 전치사는 명사나 대명사 앞에 와서 시간, 장소, 위치나 방향 등을 나타내요.

My jacket is on the bed.   나의 재킷이 침대 위에 있다.
　　　　　　위치: ~ 위에

☆ 전치사는 수단, 방법 등을 나타내기도 하고, 일반동사와 함께 쓰여 관용적인 표현으로 쓰이기도 해요.

Look at the clock.   시계를 보라.
일반동사＋전치사

전치사는 주로 명사나 대명사 앞에 오며, 전치사 뒤에 오는 대명사는 목적격이에요.
「전치사＋명사/대명사」는 전치사구라고 하며, 형용사구, 부사구, 명사구로 쓰여요.

Winky goes to school with Pinky. 윙키는 핑키와 함께 학교에 간다.
　　　　　　　　　　　전치사＋명사

Many books are on the desk. 많은 책들이 책상 위에 있다.
　　　　　　　　　전치사＋명사

> **전치사구**
> 전치사＋명사/대명사

전치사는 시간, 장소, 위치, 방향 등을 나타내요.

(1) 시간을 나타내는 전치사

전치사	뜻	전치사	뜻
at	～에: 짧은 시간, 시점	on	～에: 정해진 때, 날짜, 요일
in	～에: 비교적 긴 시간인 주, 월, 계절, 년		
before	～ 전에: 어느 때보다 이전의 시점	after	～ 후에: 어느 때보다 이후의 시점
during	～ 동안에: 행사, 사건	for	～ 동안에: 구체적 기간

(2) 장소·위치를 나타내는 전치사

전치사	뜻	전치사	뜻
at	～에서: 비교적 좁은 장소	in	～ 안에서: 비교적 넓은 장소
on	～ 위에: 표면에 닿은 위에	above	～ 위쪽에: over보다 더 위에
over	～ 바로 위에: 표면에서 조금 떨어진 위에		
under	～ 바로 아래에: 표면에서 조금 떨어진 아래에		
in front of	～ 앞에	behind	～의 뒤에
next to	～ 옆에		

(3) 방향을 나타내는 전치사

전치사	뜻	전치사	뜻
into	～ 안으로: 밖에서 안으로	up	～ 위쪽으로
out of	～에서 밖으로: 안에서 밖으로	down	～ 아래쪽으로
to	～로, ～쪽으로: 도달점이나 방향	through	～을 관통하여
along	～을 따라서	across	～을 가로질러

 전치사를 찾아 동그라미 하고, 시간, 장소·위치 중 무엇을 나타내는지 쓰세요.

1. The pencil case is on the desk. ....

2. Winky is not ready at eight twenty. ....

그 외 전치사와 관용표현

 그 외에 많이 쓰이는 전치사들은 다음과 같아요.

전치사	뜻
with	~을 가지고, ~와 함께: 수단, 방법
by	~로: 수단
without	~ 없이

> by가 이동수단을 표현할 때는 관사를 쓰지 않아요.
> by a bus (×)
> → by bus (○)
> by a train (×)
> → by train (○)

 전치사가 동사나 형용사 등과 같이 쓰여서 하나의 뜻을 이루는 관용표현도 있어요.

(1) 동사+전치사

동사+전치사	뜻
listen **to**	~을 듣다
look **at**	~을 보다
look **for**	~을 찾다
get **on**	~을 타다
get **off**	~에서 내리다
wait **for**	~을 기다리다

(2) be동사+형용사+전치사

be동사+형용사+전치사	뜻
be kind **to**	~에게 친절을 베풀다
be late **for**	~에 늦다
be good **at**	~을 잘하다
be afraid **of**	~을 무서워하다

 전치사가 들어간 관용표현에 동그라미 하고, 그 뜻을 쓰세요.

1. Winky looks at the clock. ....

2. He is late for school. ....

Story **G**rammar 전치사와 전치사가 들어간 관용표현을 찾아 쓰세요.

Winky is good at swimming. He always swims in the swimming pool. But he has a cold. He goes to the hospital with Pinky. Winky is afraid of getting an injection. Pinky looks at him very sadly.

* *get an injection* 주사 맞다

1. 전치사 ....
2. 전치사가 들어간 관용표현 ....

A 보기처럼 시간을 나타내는 전치사를 찾아 동그라미 하고, 전치사가 들어간 구의 뜻을 쓰세요.

> Winky goes to the swimming pool (at) 7 o'clock.   7시에

competition 대회
practice 연습하다
on + 요일s ~요일마다
participate in
~에 참여하다
improve 향상되다

1. There is a swimming competition in July. ....

2. Winky practices swimming on Mondays. ....

3. He swims for two hours. ....

4. He participates in a swimming camp during the vacation. ....

5. His swimming improves after his swimming lessons.
....

B 문장과 일치하는 그림을 찾아 연결하세요.

swimming suit
수영복
above ~ 위에
in front of ~ 앞에
under ~ 아래에
behind ~ 뒤에

1. My swimming suit is on the desk. ·

2. My picture is above the desk. ·

3. My box is in front of the desk. ·

4. My bag is under the desk. ·

5. Dinky is behind the desk. ·

6. My chair is next to the desk. ·

C 밑줄 친 부분의 뜻을 쓰세요.

1. Winky goes to the swimming pool <u>with Dinky</u>.

   whistle
   호루라기 소리, 휘파람

   ....

2. They go to the swimming pool together <u>by bus</u>.

   ....

3. They <u>get on</u> the bus.   ....

4. He doesn't swim <u>without his swimming cap</u>.

   ....

5. He <u>looks for</u> his swimming cap.   ....

6. He <u>listens to</u> the whistle.   ....

7. Winky's teacher <u>waits for</u> him.   ....

D 장소와 방향을 나타내는 전치사를 포함한 전치사구를 찾아 밑줄을 긋고, 그 뜻을 쓰세요.

in ~ 안에
out of ~ 밖에
hug 안다
across ~을 가로질러
along ~을 따라서

1. Dinky sleeps in the box.   ....

2. He is out of the box.   ....

3. He climbs on the bed to hug Winky.   ....

4. Winky runs down the steps.   ....

5. He runs across the sofa.   ....

6. They walk along the walls together.   ....

Quiz Time
기본튼튼

 전치사를 찾아 밑줄을 긋고, 그 밑에 시간 전치사는 '시', 장소 전치사는 '장', 방향 전치사는 '방'이라고 쓰세요.

crosswalk 횡단보도

1. Winky goes to school after his swimming lesson.

2. He has math, science, and English on Monday.

3. There are many bags on the desks.

4. His bag is next to Pinky's bag.

5. He walks across the crosswalk.

6. He runs down the hallway to his classroom.

7. His friends are playing in the classroom.

 그림과 일치하면 T, 일치하지 않으면 F에 동그라미 하세요.

Winky has a cold because he swam too much. He goes to the nurse's office.

1. Winky is standing at the door. T F

2. A desk is behind the bed. T F

3. A bag is under the desk. T F

4. Some books are on the bookshelf. T F

5. A ball is in front of the bed. T F

형광펜 쫘~악

at은 좁은 장소
at the airport

in은 넓은 장소
in Seoul

C 단어나 구를 바르게 배열하여 문장을 완성하세요.

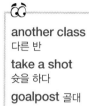

another class
다른 반

take a shot
슛을 하다

goalpost 골대

win 이기다

1. watches | his | classmates | Winky | the window | through

   ➡ _____ .

2. the playground | They | on | are

   ➡ _____ .

3. play soccer | with | They | another class

   ➡ _____ .

4. for | play | They | thirty minutes | soccer

   ➡ _____ .

5. His friend | over | takes | the goalpost | a shot

   ➡ _____ .

6. the game | His class | without | wins | him

   ➡ _____ .

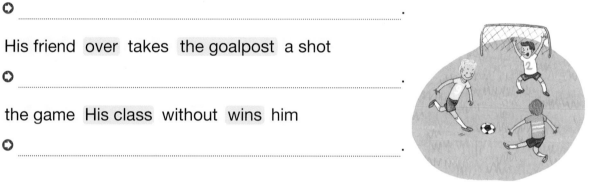

D 알맞은 전치사에 동그라미 하세요.

1. Winky listens (to / in) Pinky's voice.

2. Pinky and his friends look (during / for) him.

3. They find him and look (at / for) him sadly.

4. They are kind (with / to) him.

5. They wait (for / by) Winky to help him get home.

6. Pinky is good (on / at) swimming, too.

7. She is late (with / for) the swimming lesson.

 틀린 부분을 찾아 고쳐서 문장을 다시 쓰세요.

1. Winky goes to see a doctor in Pinky.

   ➡ ....

2. They go to the hospital to taxi.

   ➡ ....

3. The taxi passes with the tunnel.

   ➡ ....

4. They slowly walk through the crosswalk.

   ➡ ....

5. The hospital is to the third floor.

   ➡ ....

6. Winky is afraid to getting an injection.

   ➡ ....

go to see a doctor
병원에 가다
tunnel 터널
third floor 3층

 그림을 보고, 물음에 알맞은 답을 완성하세요.

1. Where is the bag?   ➡ It's ....

2. Where is the book?   ➡ It's ....

3. Where is the pillow?   ➡ It's ....

4. Where is the small chair? ➡ It's ....

5. Where is the picture?   ➡ It's ....

pillow 베개

C 의사 선생님의 처방전입니다. 보기에서 빈칸에 알맞은 전치사를 골라 쓰고, 물음에 답하세요.

at	on	for	before	after	next to

- Wash your hands .... school.
- Take a rest .... two weeks without swimming.
- Drink hot water .... bed.
- Take some medicine .... 8 o'clock.
- Go to see the doctor again .... April 5.
- The pharmacy is .... the library.

1. When does Winky wash his hands?

   ○ ....

2. How long does Winky take a rest without swimming?

   ○ ....

3. When does Winky drink hot water?

   ○ ....

4. When does Winky take some medicine?

   ○ ....

5. When is Winky going to see the doctor again?

   ○ ....

6. Where is the pharmacy?

   ○ ....

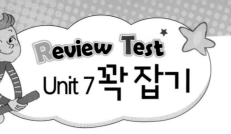

1. 다음 중 설명이 **틀린** 것을 고르세요.

① 전치사는 명사나 대명사 앞에 놓인다.

② 전치사 뒤에는 대명사의 소유격이 온다.

③ 전치사는 위치를 나타내기도 한다.

④ 전치사구는 전치사와 명사를 뜻한다.

2. 다음 중 밑줄 친 전치사의 종류가 **다른** 것을 고르세요.

① I always go to school <u>at</u> 8 o'clock.

② She is sleeping <u>during</u> the movie.

③ My uncle lives <u>in</u> New York.

④ Christmas Day is <u>on</u> December 25.

3. 다음 중 **틀린** 문장을 고르세요.

① He runs through the tunnel.　② She is leaving on Friday.

③ I work in a bank.　④ They look at his.

4. 그림과 일치하는 문장을 고르세요.

① The bird is flying over the roof.

② The bird is flying through the roof.

③ The bird is flying down the roof.

④ The bird is flying to the roof.

5. 다음을 읽고, 알맞은 그림을 직접 그리세요.

My ball is in front of the table.

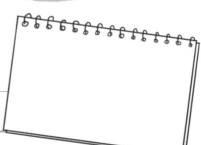

6. 다음 중 빈칸에 공통으로 알맞은 것을 고르세요.

> • I was born _____ 2002.
> • Her pencil was _____ the bag.

① in   ② at   ③ on   ④ up

7. 다음 중 빈칸에 알맞은 전치사가 순서대로 바르게 짝지어진 것을 고르세요.

> • I am waiting _____ the bus.
> • I am standing _____ the bus stop.

① by – at   ② for – at   ③ for – to   ④ to – in

8. 그림을 보고, 빈칸에 알맞은 것을 고르세요.

> She gets _____ the bus.

① in   ② on   ③ for   ④ off

9. 다음 대화에서 <u>잘못된</u> 것을 고르세요.

> Boy: Look ① <u>at</u> him. He is getting ② <u>on</u> the bus.
>
> Girl: He is my teacher.
>
> Boy: He helps poor children a lot ③ <u>with</u> some of the students.
>
> Girl: He is kind ④ <u>for</u> people.

10. 다음 중 밑줄 친 부분을 <u>잘못</u> 고친 것을 고르세요.

① He is alone <u>with</u> his mom. ⭕ He is alone without his mom.

② I'm afraid <u>in</u> that big dog. ⭕ I'm afraid on that big dog.

③ My sister listens <u>by</u> him. ⭕ My sister listens to him.

④ Let's go skiing <u>at</u> winter. ⭕ Let's go skiing in winter.

아플 땐 뭐라고 말하지?

I feel itchy all over my body.
온 몸이 가려워요.

I got stung by a mosquito.
모기에 물렸어요.

I have heavy feeling in my chest.
가슴이 답답해요.

I cut my finger with a knife.
칼에 손가락을 베었어요.

I have a puffy face.
얼굴이 부었어요.

I feel dizzy.
어지러워요.

I broke my leg.
다리가 부러졌어요.

I feel like vomiting.
토할 거 같아요.

I have a nose bleed.
코피가 나요.

My eyes are red.
눈이 충혈되었어요.

I have decayed teeth.
충치가 있어요.

조동사 can과 will

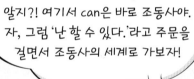

I can do it. 이 무슨 뜻인지
알지?! 여기서 can은 바로 조동사야.
자, 그럼 '난 할 수 있다.'라고 주문을
걸면서 조동사의 세계로 가보자!

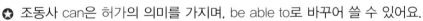

✪ 조동사 can은 허가의 의미를 가지며, be able to로 바꾸어 쓸 수 있어요.

Winky can swim. 윙키는 수영을 할 수 있다.
= is able to

✪ 조동사 will은 앞으로 일어날 미래의 일을 추측할 때 쓰이며, be going to로
바꾸어 쓸 수 있어요.

This summer will be very hot. 이번 여름은 매우 더울 것이다.
= is going to

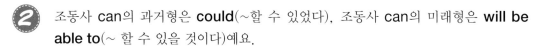
조동사 can의 용법

1 조동사는 동사를 도와주는 역할을 하는데, **can**과 **will** 등이 있어요. 조동사는 항상 같은 형태로 쓰이며 뒤에는 동사원형이 와요. 조동사 **can**은 '~할 수 있다'라는 의미로 가능성을 나타내며, **be able to**와 바꾸어 쓸 수 있어요.

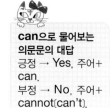

(1) **평서문**   주어 + can + 동사원형 ~.: …는 ~할 수 있다.

I can speak Chinese.   나는 중국어를 말할 수 있다.
<u>조동사 can + 동사원형</u>

(2) **부정문**   주어 + cannot(can't) + 동사원형 ~.: …는 ~할 수 없다.

He can't speak Chinese.   그는 중국어를 말할 수 없다.
<u>조동사 can't + 동사원형</u>

(3) **의문문**   Can + 주어 + 동사원형 ~?: …는 ~할 수 있니?

Can you speak Chinese?   당신은 중국어를 말할 수 있습니까?
<u>조동사 can</u> <u>동사원형</u>

○ **Yes, I can.**   네, 할 수 있습니다. / **No, I can't.**   아니요, 못합니다.

>
> **can**으로 물어보는
> 의문문의 대답
> 긍정 → Yes, 주어 +
> can.
> 부정 → No, 주어 +
> cannot(can't).

2 조동사 **can**의 과거형은 **could**(~할 수 있었다), 조동사 **can**의 미래형은 **will be able to**(~ 할 수 있을 것이다)예요.

(1) **과거 부정문**   주어 + could not(couldn't) + 동사원형 ~.: …는 ~할 수 없었다.

I couldn't go to the academy yesterday.
나는 어제 학원에 갈 수 없었다.

(2) **미래 부정문**   주어 + will not(won't) be able to + 동사원형 ~.: …는 ~할 수 없을 것이다.

I won't be able to participate in the competition.
나는 대회에 참가할 수 없을 것이다.

> 조동사 두 개는 함께
> 쓸 수 없어요. 즉, will
> can이라고는 쓰지
> 않아요.
> She *will can*
> swim this
> summer. (×)
> She **will be**
> **able to** swim
> this summer. (○)

Check 조동사에 동그라미 하고, 문장의 우리말 뜻을 쓰세요.

1. I can wake up at 6 in the morning every day. ....

2. He couldn't answer the question. ....

조동사 will의 용법

1 조동사 **will**은 '~할 것이다' 또는 '~일 것이다'라는 뜻으로 미래를 나타내요.

(1) **평서문**   주어 + will + 동사원형 ~.: …는 ~할 것이다.

The academy bus will arrive on time.
학원 버스는 제시간에 도착할 것이다.

(2) 부정문　주어 + will not(won't) + 동사원형 ~.: …는 ~하지 않을 것이다.

The academy bus will not(won't) arrive on time.

학원 버스는 제시간에 도착하지 않을 것이다.

(3) 의문문　Will + 주어 + 동사원형 ~?: …는 ~할 겁니까?

Will the academy bus **arrive** on time?

학원 버스는 제시간에 도착할 겁니까?

will로 물어보는
의문문의 대답
긍정 → Yes, 주어 +
will.
부정 → No, 주어 +
won't.

 조동사 will은 be going to로 바꾸어 쓸 수 있어요. be동사는 주어의 인칭과 수에
따라 변해요.

(1) 평서문　주어 + be동사 + going to + 동사원형 ~.

I am going to plan my summer vacation.

나는 여름방학 계획을 짤 것이다.

(2) 부정문　주어 + be동사 + not going to + 동사원형 ~.

I am not going to play computer games.

나는 컴퓨터 게임을 하지 않을 것이다.

(3) 의문문　be동사 + 주어 + going to + 동사원형 ~?

Are you going to wake up early tomorrow?

당신은 내일 일찍 일어날 겁니까?

주어가 I인 경우
am going to +
동사원형

주어가 You, We,
They인 경우
are going to +
동사원형

주어가 He, She, It
인 경우
is going to +
동사원형

be going to를
이용한 의문문의 대답
긍정 → Yes, 주어 +
be동사.
부정 → No, 주어 +
be동사 + not.

 조동사에 동그라미 하고, 문장의 우리말 뜻을 쓰세요.

1. I will visit my grandparents. ....

2. It will be very hot this summer. ....

 조동사에 동그라미 하고, 밑줄 친 문장을 긍정문과 의문문으로 고쳐 쓰세요.

Pinky is planning her summer vacation. ¹⁾She can't
swim. So she's trying to learn to swim. She will go to the
department store this weekend. She will buy a swimming
suit there. ²⁾She will be able to swim after this summer.

* *department store* 백화점

1. 긍정문 ....

2. 의문문 ....

 알맞은 동사를 찾아 동그라미 하세요.

1. Winky can (cut / cuts) a carrot into big slices.

2. Can he (stirs / stir) the cream?

3. Can Mom (peel / peels) the potatoes?

4. She can (grill / grills) the steak.

5. Can Dad (drinks / drink) some juice?

6. Can he (boil / boils) the water?

7. Dinky can (makes / make) salad dressing.

cut ~ into big slices
~을 굵직굵직하게 썰다
stir 휘젓다, 뒤섞다
peel 껍질을 벗기다
grill 석쇠에 굽다
boil 끓이다
salad dressing
샐러드 소스

B 다음을 과거형 문장으로 바꾸어 다시 쓰세요.

1. Pinky can turn on the gas.

   ○ ....

2. She can cook Korean traditional food.

   ○ ....

3. Winky can eat spicy food.

   ○ ....

4. He can eat vegetables.

   ○ ....

5. He can help his dad do the dishes.

   ○ ....

turn on ~을 켜다
traditional food
전통 음식
spicy food 매운 음식
vegetable 야채
do the dishes
설거지를 하다

그림을 보고, 빈칸에 **will** 또는 **won't**를 넣으세요.

sunglasses 선글라스
beach 해변
sandcastle 모래성
a lot 많이

1. It _____ be very hot tomorrow.

2. I _____ buy any sunglasses.

3. I _____ go to the beach in summer.

4. I _____ read a book on the beach.

5. She _____ build a sandcastle with sand.

6. It _____ rain a lot in the afternoon.

D 다음을 〔   〕 안의 문장으로 고쳐 다시 쓰세요.

vacation
homework 방학 숙제
clay 찰흙
take a shower
샤워하다
go to bed
잠자리에 들다

1. Winky will do his vacation homework.

➡ 〔부정문〕 _____

2. He will build a house with clay.

➡ 〔부정문〕 _____

3. He will go out to eat after he does his homework.

➡ 〔의문문〕 _____

4. He will take a shower.

➡ 〔의문문〕 _____

5. He will go to bed at 9.

➡ 〔의문문〕 _____

 보기와 같이 문장을 바꿔 쓸 때 빈칸에 알맞은 말을 쓰세요.

> Pinky can swim. ➡ Pinky <u>is able to</u> swim.

1. You can't jump rope.

   ➡ You ＿＿＿＿＿＿＿＿＿＿ jump rope.

2. Mom can't drive well.

   ➡ Mom ＿＿＿＿＿＿＿＿＿ drive well.

3. Dad can speak English very well.

   ➡ Dad ＿＿＿＿＿＿＿＿＿ speak English very well.

4. Dinky can read a newspaper.

   ➡ Dinky ＿＿＿＿＿＿＿＿＿ read a newspaper.

B 밑줄 친 부분을 지시대로 바꾸어 쓸 때 빈칸에 알맞은 말을 쓰세요.

1. Winky <u>can watch</u> TV at night.

   ➡ 미래형 Winky ＿＿＿＿＿＿＿＿＿ TV at night.

2. Mom <u>can wake up</u> early in the morning.

   ➡ 과거 부정형 Mom ＿＿＿＿＿＿＿＿＿ early in the morning.

3. Dad <u>can cook</u> Chinese food.

   ➡ 과거형 Dad ＿＿＿＿＿＿＿＿＿ Chinese food.

4. Pinky <u>can make</u> her bed.

   ➡ 미래형 Pinky ＿＿＿＿＿＿＿＿＿ her bed.

5. We <u>can take care of</u> Dinky and Minky.

   ➡ 과거형 We ＿＿＿＿＿＿＿＿＿ Dinky and Minky.

Chinese food
중국 음식
make one's bed
잠자리를 정돈하다
take care of
～을 돌보다

C 보기에서 알맞은 말을 골라 조동사와 함께 빈칸에 쓰세요.

> be   gather   spend   be sold   watch

1. 너는 여름방학을 어떻게 보낼 거니?

   ○ How _____ you _____ your vacation time?

2. 우리는 올 여름에 공포영화를 볼 것이다.

   ○ We _____ _____ a horror movie this summer.

3. 이번 여름은 무척 더울 것이다.

   ○ It _____ _____ very hot this summer.

4. 해변가에는 관광객이 많이 모일 것이다.

   ○ Many travelers _____ _____ at the beach.

5. 선풍기가 많이 팔릴 것이다.

   ○ A lot of electric fans _____ _____ .

D 다음 주 스케줄표를 보고, **be going to**를 사용하여 문장을 완성하세요.

Mon	Tue	Wed	Thur	Fri	Sat	Sun
do taekwondo	watch a movie	go swimming	study English	do my homework	go hiking	take a rest

1. I _____ on Monday.

2. I _____ with Jane on Tuesday.

3. _____ you _____ on Wednesday?

4. I _____ on Thursday.

5. _____ you _____ on Friday?

A 보기와 같이 빈칸을 채워 문장을 완성하세요.

> Dinky couldn't read a book last summer, but he can read now.

Chinese 중국어
ride a motorcycle
오토바이를 타다
air conditioner
에어컨

1. He couldn't play the piano last summer,

    but .... now.

2. Mom couldn't cook well last summer,

    but .... now.

3. Dad couldn't speak Chinese last summer,

    but .... now.

4. Minky couldn't ride a motorcycle well last summer,

    but .... now.

5. My parents couldn't buy an air conditioner last year,

    but .... now.

B 보기에서 알맞은 단어를 골라 조동사와 함께 빈칸에 쓰세요.

> lend   go   make   walk   ride   pitch

lend 빌려주다
pitch (천막을) 치다
have a cramp
쥐가 나다
sun block
자외선 차단제
make dinner
저녁 식사를 준비하다

1. I had a cramp in my leg. So I .... (과거 불가능)

2. You .... into the ocean. (현재 불가능)

3. .... you .... me some sun block? (부탁)

4. You .... a bicycle next year. (미래 가능)

5. I .... a tent at the beach last summer. (과거 가능)

6. .... you .... dinner for me? (공손한 부탁)

형광펜 쫘~악

can을 사용한 의문문은
부탁의 뜻을 나타내기도
해요. can 대신에 could를
사용하면 더욱 공손한
부탁 표현이 되지요.
Could you ~?: ~해주
실 수 있을까요?

다음 주 일기 예보를 읽고, 밑줄 친 부분을 바르게 고쳐 쓰세요.

1) It was clear on Monday. It will be a little hot, so wear short sleeves.

2) It will be sunny, and the temperature will drop on Tuesday.

Since it will rain on Wednesday and Thursday, 3) you need an umbrella.

4) It will rain on Friday.

5) The temperature went up on Saturday and Sunday. You must have sunglasses or a parasol.

Mon	Tue	Wed	Thur	Fri	Sat	Sun

1. ....

2. ....

3. ....

4. ....

5. ....

1. 다음 중 우리말에 맞게 빈칸에 알맞은 말을 고르세요.

> 문을 닫아 주실 수 있을까요?
>
> ❍ _____ you close the door?

① Are   ② Could   ③ Can't   ④ Won't

2. 다음 그림을 보고, 빈칸에 알맞은 조동사를 고르시오.

> She _____ play the violin yesterday.

① can   ② can't   ③ could   ④ couldn't

3. 다음 중 빈칸에 알맞은 것을 고르세요.

> Dad _____ go on a business trip to New York next week.

① is   ② does   ③ will   ④ was

4. 다음 중 빈칸에 알맞은 것을 고르세요.

> It _____ rain tomorrow.

① wasn't   ② don't   ③ doesn't   ④ won't

5. 다음 중 틀린 문장을 고르세요.

① I couldn't swim.   ② She can win the game.
③ He'll can win the game.   ④ Can he make a paper airplane?

6. 다음 중 <u>틀린</u> 문장을 고르세요.

① He's going to be thirteen next year.
② It's not going to snow in Seoul this Christmas.
③ I'm going to have breakfast at 11 tomorrow.
④ Will you going to go to Italy next summer vacation?

7. 다음 질문에 맞는 답을 찾아 바르게 연결하세요.

1) Can you play baseball?   ·   · No, I'm not.
2) Are you going to swim this weekend? ·   · No, it won't
3) Will it snow tomorrow?   ·   · Yes, I can.

8. 보기에서 알맞은 조동사를 골라 빈칸에 알맞게 바꿔 쓰세요.

can	could	can't	couldn't

1) _____ a dog fly? ➡ No, it can't.

2) She _____ pass the test last year.

3) _____ you pass me the salt?

4) I _____ hear you talk. Can you raise your voice?

9. 다음 빈칸에 **be going to**를 알맞게 넣어 문장을 완성하세요.

1) I _____ study English on Wednesday.

2) He _____ have a birthday party this Sunday.

10. 다음 중 올바른 문장을 고르세요.

① He will be able to sing on stage tomorrow.
② People can't travel in space in the past.
③ I'll be going to attend camp this vacation.
④ She will comes to the concert.

공손한 표현

우리말에만 존댓말이 있다구요? No! 영어에도 존댓말과 반말이 있답니다. 영어권 나라에서는 나이나 지위 말고도 상황에 따라 존댓말을 써요. 일반적으로 please를 쓰거나 would, could를 사용해서 말해요.

상대방의 말을 잘못 알아 들었을 때

- **I'm sorry. Would you mind repeating that?**
  죄송하지만 다시 한 번 말씀해 주시겠어요?

- **Would you repeat that, please?**
  다시 한 번 말씀해 주시겠어요?

초대할 때

- **Would you like to come to my house?**
  제 집으로 와 주시겠어요?

- **Please help yourselves.**
  마음껏 드세요.

요청 또는 허락 받기

- **Could I use your phone?**
  당신의 전화를 좀 써도 될까요?

- **Could I ask some questions?**
  질문 좀 해도 될까요?

정답 및 해설

과거동사

be동사와 일반동사의 과거형 check p.14

He saw a map on the wall.
그는 벽에 걸린 지도를 보았다.

be동사와 일반동사 과거형의 부정문과 의문문 check p.15

1. Dad wasn't in the kitchen.
2. Did he cook spaghetti?

Story Grammar

1. prepared, packed, looked, wasn't, asked, Did, answered, was
2. · His bag didn't look heavy.
   · Was she at school?

🌐 윙키는 그의 여행을 준비했어요. 그는 가방을 쌌어요. 그의 가방은 무거워 보였어요. 핑키는 집에 없었어요. 엄마가 윙키에게 물었어요. "핑키를 학교에서 보았니?" 윙키가 대답했어요. "네. 그녀는 학교에 있었어요."

Quiz Time 기초 탄탄 p.16

A 1. worked   2. looked   3. liked
   4. stopped   5. cried   6. walked
   7. studied   8. answered
   9. was   10. were   11. was   12. did
   13. wrote   14. made   15. took   16. got

B 1. went   2. was   3. were   4. had
   5. looked   6. ate   7. cooked

C 1. wasn't   2. didn't   3. weren't   4. didn't
   5. didn't   6. wasn't   7. didn't   8. didn't
   9. weren't

D 1. Were   2. Were   3. Was   4. Did
   5. Did   6. Was   7. Were   8. Did
   9. Did   10. Were

Quiz Time 기본 튼튼 p.18

A 1. He **was** at Times Square yesterday.
   2. He **found** a fun place.
   3. People **were** very busy.
   4. They **walked** very fast.
   5. He **ate** ice cream.

B 1. She brushed her teeth.
   2. I watched a movie.
   3. I played baseball.
   4. Steve met his friends.
   5. I cut the paper with scissors.
   6. I read a book.
   7. She was happy.
   8. They went home.

C 1. didn't ride   2. didn't talk
   3. didn't move   4. wasn't
   5. didn't arrive

D 1. Was he thirsty?
   2. Was the river big and beautiful?
   3. Did Mom do an experiment?
   4. Did the water become drinkable?
   5. Were they very happy?

📖 **해설**

D 3. 일반동사가 쓰인 과거형 문장을 의문문으로 고칠 때는 「Did＋주어＋동사원형 ～?」의 순서로 쓴다.

Quiz Time 실력 쑥쑥 p.20

A 1. woke   2. ate   3. was   4. left
   5. went   6. were

B 1. lived   2. made   3. danced   4. shook

C 1. Yes, he cleaned his room.
   2. No, he didn't fight with his younger sibling.
   3. No, he didn't wash his hands in the bathroom.
   4. Yes, he wrote in his diary at night.
   5. No, he didn't save money.
   6. Yes, he had a wonderful day.

Review Test Unit 1 꽉 잡기 p.22

1. ④   2. ③   3. listened   4. ③
5. ②   6. ③   7. ①   8. ③   9. ①
10. ③

📖 **해설**

2. am, love, get은 모두 현재동사이다.
3. listen은 「단모음＋단자음」으로 끝이 나지만 앞 음절에 강세가 오므로 예외적으로 마지막 자음을 하나 더 붙이지 않고 끝에 -ed만 붙인다.
4. He는 3인칭 단수주어이므로 be동사 is의 과거형인 was를 써야 한다.

5. yesterday는 '어제'라는 뜻으로 과거동사와 함께 쓴다.

8. be동사로 물어보면 be동사로 대답한다.

2 현재진행형과 과거진행형

현재진행형 Check p.26

1. Are you studying now?
너는 지금 공부하는 중이니?

2. No. I am watching baseball.
아니오. 전 야구를 보는 중이에요.

과거진행형 Check p.27

1. Were   **2.** Was

Story Grammar

Winky and his friend, Steve like baseball. They are playing baseball. Winky is throwing the ball. Steve hits the ball and is running very fast.

1. They were playing baseball.

2. Were they playing baseball?

🌐 윙키와 그의 친구 스티브는 야구를 좋아해요.
그들은 야구를 하는 중이에요.
윙키가 공을 던져요.
스티브는 공을 치고 아주 빠르게 달려가고 있어요.

Quiz time 기초 탄탄 p.28

A 1. is watching   2. is looking
3. is pulling   4. is standing
5. is giving   6. is waving

B 1. is not   2. is not   3. is not   4. is not
5. is not   6. is not   7. are not

C 1. was going   2. were waiting
3. were watching   4. was throwing
5. was running   6. was screaming

D 1. Were   2. Were   3. Was   4. Was
5. Was   6. Was   7. Was

Quiz time 기본 튼튼 p.30

A 1. am not watching
2. aren't singing
3. aren't playing
4. aren't sitting
5. isn't shooting

B 1. Is one player passing
2. Is the referee blowing
3. Is the coach shouting
4. Are the players going
5. Are they drinking

C 1. was watching   2. were entering
3. was passing   4. was hitting
5. was giving

D 1. Were, playing   2. was raining
3. were, doing   4. was sleeping

Quiz time 실력 쑥쑥 p.32

A 1. Winky and Pinky are playing soccer with their family.
2. Winky is running toward the goal.
3. He is kicking the ball.
4. Dad is blocking the ball.

B 1. (부정문) Dinky isn't running toward Mom.
(의문문) Is Dinky running toward Mom?
(과거진행형) Dinky was running toward Mom.
2. (부정문) Dinky isn't holding a ball in his mouth.
(의문문) Is Dinky holding a ball in his mouth?
(과거진행형) Dinky was holding a ball in his mouth.

C 1. He is doing his homework.
2. No, he isn't. (He is taking a rest and planning to play tennis with his sister.)
3. No, he wasn't. (He was playing tennis with his dad.)
4. He is planning to play tennis with his sister.

Review Test Unit 2 꽉 잡기 p.34

1. ③   **2.** ②   **3.** ①   **4.** ④   **5.** ③

6. ④   **7.** ④   **8.** ③

9. 1) They are jumping.   2) She is watching them.

10. 1) He isn't running very fast.

2) I wasn't shaking hands with her.

해설

4. ③ I'm not going home yesterday.에서 yesterday는 과거를 나타내는 단어로 현재진행을 나타내는 표현에 쓰면 어색하다.

8. ① 현재진행형에 '어제'라는 과거를 나타내는 단어를 쓴 것이 어색하다.
② 현재진행형으로 만들려면 doesn't를 aren't로 고쳐야 한다.
④ is를 are로 고쳐야 맞다.

Unit 3 형용사와 부사

형용사의 종류와 용법 Check p.38

1. interesting ◑ 서술적 용법
2. red ◑ 제한적 용법
beautiful ◑ 서술적 용법

부사의 종류와 위치 Check p.39

Pinky studies English (very) (hard). She is (often) late for school.

Story Grammar

1. many, happy, big, green, long, new
2. very, quickly

☺ 윙키의 생일이에요. 윙키의 친구들은 그를 위해 생일파티를 열어요. 그는 많은 선물을 받아서 매우 행복해요. 그는 큰 초록색 상자를 재빨리 열어요. 그 상자 안에는 긴 새 마법 지팡이가 있어요.

Quiz Time 기초 탄탄 p.40

A 1. It was a (small) room. 작은
2. Winky was sleeping in his (old) bed. 오래된
3. His friends gave him (ten) presents. 10개의
4. He was around (many) presents. 많은
5. But that was his (sweet) dream. 달콤한
6. He is very (excited) about his birthday.
흥분한, 신난

B 1. 서술적 용법   2. 제한적 용법   3. 제한적 용법
4. 서술적 용법   5. 제한적 용법   6. 서술적 용법
7. 제한적 용법

C 1. Let's go to the magic shop (quickly). 재빨리
2. They (happily) go to the magic shop (together).
행복하게 / 함께
3. Does he like to read books (much)? 많이
4. He (sometimes) reads books. 때때로
5. His magic wand is old (now). 지금
6. He wants a magic cape (very) (much). 매우, 많이

D 1. Pinky makes a pretty ribbon very well.
2. Make the ribbon quickly, Pinky.
3. Wait! I'm making the ribbon fast.
4. Everyone, talk quietly, please.
5. Winky usually gets home early.
6. Luckily, he is cleaning the classroom at school.

Quiz Time 기본 튼튼 p.42

A 1. Pinky decorates her room with **twenty balloons** today.
2. They bake **something delicious**.
3. She buys **beautiful flowers**.
4. She is very excited about his **big birthday party**.
5. They quickly wrap Winky's present with two **red ribbons**.

B 1. Pinky is my kind sister.
2. This birthday cake is delicious.
3. She bakes sweet cookies.
4. Fifteen red and yellow flowers are beautiful.
5. A friend buys something special.

C 1. Everyone **often** takes an English exam.
2. They **always** study English very hard.
3. Winky is **usually** very excited to study English.
4. His friends **never** celebrate his birthday.
5. They **sometimes** talk each other in English.

D 1. happily   2. quietly   3. pleasantly
4. quickly   5. Suddenly   6. slowly

A 1. Here is your blue birthday hat.
2. There are twenty balloons.
3. Here is your round plate.
4. Winky eats delicious cookies.

B 1. well 2. fast 3. perfectly 4. much

C 1. Let's play the piñata game **quickly**.
2. It's Winky's turn. Winky **carefully** covers his eyes.
3. He hits the piñata very **hard** with a stick.
4. **Suddenly**, the piñata breaks and they get some sweet candy.

D 1. It was sunny.
2. He ate five cookies.
3. He got a long new magic wand and a magic cape.

Review Test Unit 3 꽉 잡기 p.46

1. ④ 2. ③ 3. ① 4. ③ 5. ②
6. ② 7. ④ 8. ② 9. ④ 10. ②

해설

1. -thing으로 끝나는 명사는 형용사가 뒤에서 꾸민다.
2. ①, ②, ④의 형용사는 서술적 용법이고, ③의 형용사는 제한적 용법으로 쓰였다.
3. often, usually, always는 빈도부사이다.
4. 빈도부사는 조동사와 be동사 뒤, 일반동사 앞에 놓는다.
6. little은 '작은,' a little은 '약간'이라는 뜻이다.
7. ④의 very는 well을 꾸며준다.
9. 빈칸에는 car를 꾸며주는 형용사가 와야 한다.

Unit 4 비교급과 최상급

형용사와 부사의 비교급과 최상급 Check p.50

1. old / older / oldest 더 나이 많은 / 가장 나이 많은
2. smaller / smallest / small 더 작은 / 가장 작은

비교급과 최상급의 활용 Check p.51

1. 비 2. 최

Winky is taller than Pinky. So Winky has a longer jump rope. Winky's cap is expensive, but Pinky's cap is more expensive. Mom's training pants are shorter than Dad's training pants. The whole family exercises together.
1. Winky has the longest jump rope.
2. Pinky's cap is the most expensive.

> 윙키는 핑키보다 키가 커요. 그래서 윙키는 더 긴 줄넘기를 가지고 있어요. 윙키의 모자는 비싸지만 핑키의 모자는 더 비싸요. 엄마의 운동복 바지는 아빠의 운동복 바지보다 짧아요. 온 가족이 함께 운동을 해요.

A 1. more expensive 2. shorter
3. smaller 4. more 5. cleaner
6. thicker 7. lighter 8. higher

B 1. ○ 2. ○ 3. × 4. ○
5. ○ 6. ○

C 1. fatter 2. more beautiful
3. more 4. as fast as
5. easier 6. as hard as
7. happier 8. as old as

D 1. youngest 2. lightest
3. strongest 4. tallest
5. most 6. fattest
7. most popular 8. shortest

해설

A 비교급 만들기: 1음절인 형용사나 부사는 뒤에 -er을 붙인다. 2음절 이상인 형용사나 부사인 경우에는 앞에 more를 붙인다.

B 최상급 만들기: 1음절인 형용사나 부사는 뒤에 -est을 붙인다. 2음절 이상인 형용사나 부사인 경우에는 앞에 most를 붙인다.

C as+원급+as: …만큼 ~한

A 1. faster, slower 2. slower
3. longer 4. slower

B 1. the largest 2. the cheapest
3. the most interesting 4. the thinnest

C 1. Winky arrives at the gym earlier than Pinky.

(= Winky arrives earlier than Pinky at the gym.)

2. A treadmill is more expensive than a bike.
3. Pinky's sportswear is newer than Winky's.
4. Yoga is as fun as Pilates.

D warmer, happier, best, more, most popular

실력 쑥쑥 p.56

A 1. A basketball is bigger than a volleyball.
2. Soccer is more popular than baseball.
3. The ocean is colder than the swimming pool.
4. A vaulting pole is longer than a stick.

B 1. Today is the hottest day of the year.
2. He is the shortest boy in his class.
3. P.E. is the most boring class today.
4. She is the youngest teacher at my school.

C 1. more fast ⊙ faster
2. the expensivest ⊙ the most expensive
3. more smaller ⊙ smaller
4. hoter ⊙ hotter
5. slowest ⊙ slower

Review Test Unit 4 꼭 잡기 p.58

1. ③　　2. ④　　3. ③　　4. ②　　5. ③
6. ②　　7. ④
8. 1) America is further away · · than meat.
   2) Vegetables are healthier · · than Japan.
9. 1) better, than 2) smartest
10. 1) Baekdu Mountain is higher than Halla Mountain.
    2) Tom is the most handsome in his class.

🔎 해설
3. 비교급＋than＋명사／대명사: (둘 중에서) …보다 더 ~한
9. 1) be good at: ~에 능숙하다, ~을 잘하다
   good의 비교급: better

Unit 5 의문사

의문대명사와 의문형용사 Check p.62
1. What time is Willy coming?
2. Whose is this bag?

의문부사 Check p.63
1. Where is Willy?
2. How old is his dad?

Story Grammar
1. Where　　2. time

📖 오늘 윙키의 사촌이 올 거예요.
그는 뉴질랜드에 살아요. 그는 비행기를 타고 올 거예요.
그는 6시에 도착할 거예요. 윙키 가족은 4시 30분에 그를 데리러 공항으로 갈 예정이죠. 윙키 아빠는 공항까지 차를 운전해 갈 거예요.

기초 탄탄 p.64

A 1. Who　　2. Who　　3. What　　4. What
B 1. time　　2. kind　　3. book　　4. room
5. food

C 1. Why did Winky take out a magic marble?
2. What did Winky do with the magic marble?
3. Where was Willy in the marble?

D 1. ○　　2. ×　　3. ○　　4. ×
5. ○

기본 튼튼 p.66

A 1. Who　　2. Where　　3. Who(m)　　4. What
B 1. What time　　　　2. Which
3. Which　　　　4. Whose

C 1. Are, What are　　2. Are, Where are
3. Does, Who(m) does

D 1. **How** big is the bag?
2. How **many** clothes does he have?
3. How **long** does he stay at Winky's house?
4. How **much** money does he exchange?

실력 쑥쑥 p.68

A 1. ○　　2. ○　　3. ×　　4. ×

114

B 1. Where   2. What   3. What   4. Where

C 1. Where do you live?
2. What is your occupation?
3. How long are you staying in Korea?
4. How often do you come to Korea?
5. Why did you come to Korea?

해설
A 3. 윌리가 어디 출신인지는 일기에 나오지 않는다.
4. 윌리가 비행기를 얼마나 탔는지는 일기에 나오지 않는다.

1. ①   2. ②   3. ③   4. ③   5. ③
6. ②   7. ②   8. ④

9. What's his name?
10. 1) When is your birthday?
2) How much is it?

해설
4. ③ games가 복수로 표현된 셀 수 있는 명사이기 때문에 much를 many로 바꿔 써야 옳다.
7. souvenir는 '기념품'이라는 뜻의 셀 수 있는 명사이다.
8. ① What time are we meeting?이 옳은 문장이다.
② Which gate are you waiting?이 옳은 문장이다.
③ How do you go there?가 옳은 문장이다.

Unit 6 비인칭주어 it과 There is / are ~

비인칭주어 it Check p.74

1. ○   2. ○   3. ×   4. ×

There is ~와 There are ~ Check p.75

1. is   2. isn't   3. Is there
4. Are there

Story Grammar
1. 저기에 세탁기가 있다.
2. · What day is (it) today?, (It)'s Sunday., (It)'s very sunny today.
   · (It)'s very noisy.
   🌐 무슨 소리예요? 저기에 세탁기가 있어요. 와우! 매우 시끄럽네요. 오늘은 무슨 요일인가요? 오늘은 일요일이에요. 날씨는 어때요? 오늘 날씨는 매우 화창해요.

A 1. 시간   2. 계절   3. 날짜   4. 거리
5. 날씨   6. 요일   7. 명암   8. 명암

B 1. 비   2. 인   3. 인   4. 비
5. 비   6. 비   7. 비   8. 인

C 1. are   2. is   3. are   4. Is
5. aren't   6. isn't   7. are   8. are
9. is

D 1. is   2. Is   3. are   4. Is
5. is   6. is   7. isn't

A 1. It is   2. It is   3. It is   4. It is
5. It is

B 1. It **is** a quarter to nine.
2. What time **is** it?
3. It **is** far from here to go there.
4. It **is** 1 mile from the event hall.
5. **Is** it windy?

C 1. are   2. are   3. are   4. Is
5. is   6. are   7. are   8. Is
9. is

D 1. There is water in the event hall.
2. Is there a cloud?
3. Is there a lot of water now?
4. There aren't trees on the road.
5. Is there money to donate for Earth?

해설
C There is / are ~ 구문에서 단수명사 앞에는 단수동사 is를 쓴다.

A 1. It is   2. It is   3. It isn't   4. It is

B 1. It is summer.
2. Yes, it's nice. / It is hot. (그림에 맞는 날씨에 대한 설명은 모두 정답)
3. It is 9 o'clock.
4. No, it is not(isn't) dark.

C 1. are, books   2. is, dust
3. aren't, chairs   4. are, clothes

D 1. There are   2. there isn't
3. there isn't

해설

C There is ~ 뒤에는 단수명사, There are ~ 뒤에는 복수명사가 따라 나온다.

Review Test Unit 6 꼭 잡기 p.82

1. ④   **2.** ①   **3.** ③   **4.** ①   **5.** ①
6. ①   **7.** ③   **8.** ①   **9.** ②   **10.** ④

해설

1. 비인칭주어 it은 인칭이 아니라는 뜻으로 별도의 해석을 하지 않으므로 '인칭'은 정답이 아니다.

2. ① '그것은 책이다.'라는 뜻으로, 인칭주어 it을 '그것'으로 해석한다.

4. ② 2시 15분 전을 뜻하는 표현으로 1시 45분을 말한다.
     ③ quarter는 15분을 나타내는 단어로 2시 15분 전, 즉 1시 45분을 뜻한다.

7. 아래가 올바른 표현이다.
   ① There is an egg.
   ② There is a cushion on the chair.
   ④ There are 28 desks.

8. pen은 셀 수 있는 명사이므로 many(많은)와 함께 사용 할 수 있다. 나머지는 셀 수 없는 명사이므로 much(많은)를 써야 한다.

10. 아래가 올바른 표현이다.
   ① There are many cookies.
   ② There is water in the glass.
   ③ There is full of dust on the television.

Unit 7 전치사

전치사의 쓰임과 종류 Check p.86

1. The pencil case is on the desk. 장소·위치
2. Winky is not ready at eight twenty. 시간

그 외 전치사와 관용표현 Check p.87

1. Winky looks at the clock. ~을 보다
2. He is late for school. ~에 늦다

Quiz Time 기초 탄탄 p.88

A 1. in July / 7월에
     2. on Mondays / 월요일마다
     3. for two hours / 2시간 동안
     4. during the vacation / 방학 동안에
     5. after his swimming lessons / 수영 수업 후에

B 1. My swimming suit is on the desk.
     2. My picture is above the desk.
     3. My box is in front of the desk.
     4. My bag is under the desk.
     5. Dinky is behind the desk.
     6. My chair is next to the desk.

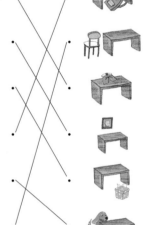

C 1. 딩키와 함께   2. 버스를 타고
     3. ~을 타다   4. 수영모자 없이
     5. ~을 찾다   6. ~을 듣다
     7. ~을 기다리다

D 1. in the box / 상자 안에
     2. out of the box / 상자 밖에
     3. on the bed / 침대 위에
     4. down the steps / 계단 아래쪽으로
     5. across the sofa / 소파를 가로질러
     6. along the walls / 벽을 따라서

Quiz Time 기본 탄탄 p.90

A 1. to, after / 방, 시   2. on / 시   3. on / 장
     4. next to / 장   5. across / 방

6. down, to / 방, 방   **7.** in / 장

B 1. T   2. F   3. F   4. T   5. T

C 1. Winky watches his classmates through the window.
2. They are on the playground.
3. They play soccer with another class.
4. They play soccer for thirty minutes.
5. His friend takes a shot over the goalpost.
6. His class wins the game without him.

D 1. to   2. for   3. at   4. to
5. for   6. at   7. for

Quiz Time 실력 쑥쑥 p.92

A 1. Winky goes to see a doctor **with** Pinky.
2. They go to the hospital **by** taxi.
3. The taxi passes **through** the tunnel.
4. They slowly walk **across** the crosswalk.
5. The hospital is **on** the third floor.
6. Winky is afraid **of** getting an injection.

B 1. under the desk
2. on the desk
3. on the bed
4. in front of the desk
5. above the bed / on the wall

C after, for, before, at, on, next to
1. Winky washes his hands after school.
2. Winky takes a rest for two weeks without swimming.
3. Winky drinks hot water before bed.
4. Winky takes some medicine at 8 o'clock.
5. Winky is going to see the doctor again on April 5.
6. The pharmacy is next to the library.

Review Test Unit 7 꼭 잡기 p.94

1. ②   2. ③   3. ④   4. ①
5. (책상 앞에 공이 있는 그림을 그릴 것) 6. ①   7. ②
8. ④   9. ④   10. ②

🔍 해설

1. 전치사 뒤에는 명사나 대명사가 나오는데, 대명사는 목적격만 쓸 수 있다.
2. ①, ②, ④는 시간 전치사이고, ③은 장소 전치사이다.
3. at은 전치사이기 때문에 대명사의 목적격 him이 와야 한다.

---

6. 첫 번째 in은 시간 전치사이고, 두 번째 in은 장소 전치사이다.

 8 조동사 can과 will

조동사 can의 용법 Check p.98

1. I (can) wake up at 6 in the morning every day.
   나는 매일 아침 6시에 일어날 수 있다.
2. He (couldn't) answer the question.
   그는 질문에 대답할 수 없었다.

조동사 will의 용법 Check p.99

1. I (will) visit my grandparents.
   나는 조부모님 댁을 방문할 것이다.
2. It (will) be very hot this summer.
   이번 여름은 매우 더울 것이다.

Story Grammar

Pinky is planning her summer vacation. She (can't) swim. So she's trying to learn to swim. She (will) go to the department store this weekend. She (will) buy a swimming suit there. She (will be able to) swim after this summer.
1. She can swim.
2. Will she be able to swim after this summer?

🌐 핑키는 그녀의 여름 방학을 계획하고 있어요. 그녀는 수영을 못해요. 그래서 그녀는 수영을 배우기 위해 노력하고 있어요. 그녀는 이번 주말에 백화점에 갈 거예요. 그녀는 거기서 수영복을 살 거예요. 그녀는 이번 여름 이후에는 수영을 할 수 있을 거예요.

Quiz Time 기초 탄탄 p.100

A 1. cut   2. stir   3. peel   4. grill
5. drink   6. boil   7. make

B 1. Pinky could turn on the gas.
2. She could cook Korean traditional food.
3. Winky could eat spicy food.
4. He could eat vegetables.
5. He could help his dad do the dishes.

C 1. will   2. won't   3. will   4. won't
5. will   6. will

D 1. Winky won't (will not) do his vacation homework.

2. He won't(will not) build a house with clay.
3. Will he go out to eat after he does his homework?
4. Will he take a shower?
5. Will he go to bed at 9?

Quiz Time 기본 튼튼 p.102

A 1. are not able to   2. is not able to
   3. is able to   4. is able to

B 1. will be able to watch
   2. couldn't wake up
   3. could cook
   4. will be able to make
   5. could take care of

C 1. will, spend   2. will watch
   3. will be   4. will gather
   5. will be sold

D 1. am going to do taekwondo
   2. am going to watch a movie
   3. Are, going to go swimming
   4. am going to study English
   5. Are, going to do your homework

Quiz Time 실력 쑥쑥 p.104

A 1. he can play the piano
   2. she can cook well
   3. he can speak Chinese
   4. she(it) can ride a motorcycle well
   5. they can buy an air conditioner

B 1. couldn't walk   2. can't go
   3. Can, lend   4. will be able to ride
   5. could pitch   6. Could, make

C 1. It will be clear on Monday.
   2. It will be cloudy
   3. you will need an umbrella
   4. It won't rain on Friday.(It will be sunny on Friday.)
   5. The temperature will go up on Saturday and Sunday.

Review Test Unit 8 꽉 잡기 p.106

1. ②   2. ③   3. ③   4. ④   5. ③

6. ④

7. 1) Can you play baseball?
   2) Are you going to swim this weekend?
   3) Will it snow tomorrow?
   • No, I'm not.
   • No, it won't.
   • Yes, I can.

8. 1) Can   2) couldn't   3) Could   4) can't

9. 1) am going to   2) is going to

10. ①

해설

1. could는 can의 과거형이지만 공손한 부탁을 나타낼 때도 쓰인다.
2. yesterday는 과거이므로 can의 과거형 could를 써야 한다.
5. can의 미래형은 will be able to이며, 조동사는 연달아 두 개를 함께 쓸 수 없다.
9. be going to에서 be동사는 주어의 인칭과 수에 따라 형태가 달라진다.
10. ① 조동사 can의 미래형은 will be able to이다.
   ② in the past는 '과거에'라는 의미이므로 couldn't travel 이 되어야 한다.
   ③ attend camp는 '캠프에 참여하다'라는 뜻이다.
   ④ 조동사 다음에는 동사원형이 온다.

WOW! Smart Grammar

와 ~스마트한 그래머 책이 나왔대!
우 리들이 문법 공부 하기에 딱인 걸! (한승연, 성남송현초)
스 르르 빠져드는
마 법 같은 문법책
트 집 잡을 곳이 하나도 없는 멋진 책! (김다희, 성남송현초)
그 래 그래 바로 이 책이야~
래 (레)몬처럼 상큼하고
머 리가 시원해지는 문법책이다! (김혜준, 신월초)

와 우! 문법을 이야기로 공부하는 책이 나온다면
우 리가 쏜살같이 달려가서 사버려야지!! (백원종, 판교초)
스 마트한 그래머 책이 나왔다고?
마 법처럼 머리에 쏙 쏙 들어 오네!
트 랄랄라 신나게 공부하자! (김한영, 판교초)
그 래머 책은 학생의 미
래 실력이 튼튼하도록
머 슴처럼 도와 줍니다. (김규빈, 성남송현초)

와 이 책은 이야기 문법책이잖아!
우 리 집에 있는 재미없는 문법책보다 훨씬 재미있네. (민규원, 내정중)
스 스로 공부하려면 작심삼일
마 음 먹은 대로 공부하게 해주는 이 책으로
트 러블투성이 빵점 짜리 시험지 앞에 10 하나 그려 넣자. (김지민, 내정중)
그 래! 할 수 있어
래 (내) 미래를 펼쳐 줄 WOW Smart Grammar!
머 어~ㅅ지게 도전해 보자! (조유진, 판교초)